Becoming *a* Woman *Who* Listens *to* God

SHARON JAYNES

HARVEST HOUSE PUBLISHERS

EUGENE, OREGON

Cover by Dugan Design Group, Bloomington, Minnesota

BECOMING A WOMAN WHO LISTENS TO GOD
Copyright © 2004 by Sharon Jaynes
Published by Harvest House Publishers
Eugene, Oregon 97402
www.harvesthousepublishers.com

ISBN 978-0-7369-4761-9 (pbk.)
ISBN 978-0-7369-4762-6 (eBook)

The Library of Congress has cataloged the edition as follows:

Library of Congress Cataloging-in-Publication Data
Jaynes, Sharon.
  Becoming a woman who listens to God / Sharon Jaynes.
    p. cm.
Includes bibliographical references.
  ISBN 978-0-7369-1350-8 (pbk.)
    1. Christian women—Religious life. 2. Listening—Religous aspects—Christianity. I. Title.
    BV4527.J384   2004
    248.8'43—dc22   2004001423

Printed in the United States of America

12   13   14   15   16   17   18   / LB-CF /   10   9   8   7   6   5   4   3   2   1

This book is dedicated to the two special men in my life.

One captured my heart the first time our eyes met at a college Bible study,
and the other the moment our eyes locked in the delivery room.
I thank God every day for the gift of you,

my husband, Steve, and son, Steven.

Acknowledgments

A special thanks to...

My friends who are mentioned in this book. My life has been enriched by knowing each of you. Thank you for allowing me to share your lives with others.

Carolyn McCready, LaRae Weikert, and Terry Glaspey of Harvest House Publishers. Your passion for sharing the hope of Jesus Christ through print is evident in all you do.

My editor, Kim Moore; managing editor, Betty Fletcher; publicist, Teresa Evenson; and cover coordinator, Barb Sherrill. Your enthusiasm is contagious and attention to detail superb. Thank you for all the hard work and many hours invested in helping others become women who listen to God.

The staff of Proverbs 31 Ministries: Lysa TerKeurst, Bonnie Schulte, Marie Ogram, Glynnis Whitwer, Shelly Chen, Barb Spenser, Sherri Killion, Laurie Webster, Van Walton, Jill Tracey, Renee Swope, and Mary Southerland. Each one of you is a woman who has her ear pressed to the heart of God. What a joy it is to serve Him with you.

My husband, Steve, and son, Steven, for enduring piles of paper and hearing stories read time and time again.

Most of all, I thank the Lord for opening my eyes to sense His presence and quickening my heart to hear His voice in ordinary life situations.

Contents

PART I

How God Speaks

GOD STILL SPEAKS TODAY

ecoming a woman who listens to God—I don't know of any greater passion or purpose that has ever taken hold of my heart. It encapsulates my deepest longing. And as I read the pages of my well-worn Bible, I see God speaking to Adam and Eve, calling them as they walked together in the cool of the evening; to Cain, warning him that sin was crouching at the door; to Noah, instructing him on how to build the ark to save his family from destruction; to Abram, promising him he would be the father of a great nation; to Rebekah, foretelling the future of the twin boys that struggled in her womb; to Moses, calling him to lead the enslaved Israelites out of Egypt and into the Promised Land; to the prophet Samuel, leading him to anoint a mere shepherd boy the next king of the Jews. I see Jesus calling out to Saul from a blinding light saying, "Saul, Saul, why do you persecute Me?"

Tell me, haven't you longed for God to speak to you in the same way?

Admittedly, it is hard to hear anyone's voice surrounded as we are by the cacophony of noises in our busy world, where the TV is blaring, the radio is booming, the washing machine is spinning, the vacuum cleaner is roaring, the kids are yelling, the dog is barking, the baby is crying, the telephone is ringing, and the doorbell is buzzing—all at the same time. I've often thought, *if I could just get away from the clamor and calamity of everyday life, perhaps I could hear that still, small voice.* But when I pored over the pages of Scripture, I discovered that some of God's most memorable messages were not delivered while men and women were away at a spiritual retreat, but right in the middle of the hustle and bustle of everyday life. He spoke to Moses while he was tending sheep, to Gideon while he was threshing wheat, to Zechariah while he was performing his duties at the temple, to shepherds while they were watching their flocks by night, to Peter and Andrew while they were fishing on the sea, to the woman at the well while she was drawing water for her household chores, to Matthew while he was busy in his tax office, and to Martha while she was baking in the kitchen.

Does that mean that God could speak to you and to me in the midst of our ordinary days? I don't believe it is a question of whether or not He will speak, but whether or not we will listen. Henry Blackaby, in his book *Experiencing God*, said, "Right now God is working all around you and in your life. One of the greatest tragedies among God's people is that, while they have a deep longing to experience God, they are experiencing God day after day, but do not know how to recognize Him."[1] I see that longing to experience God in the sea of faces when I am speaking from the podium at a conference or women's retreat. I sense that longing in the e-mails that travel to my computer screen. I read that longing in the tearstained letters that come to my mailbox. I hear that longing in the voices of women I talk to every day. I feel that longing in my own heart each morning when I step out of bed to meet a new day. *Lord, I want to hear You today.*

There are some who say that God does not speak today, that the Bible is God's complete revelation to believers. Yes, it is true that the Bible tells us everything we need to know about God's character and His ways, and He will never tell us anything that contradicts His Word. But He will speak to us in a personal way to help us apply Scripture to our lives and move the truths from our heads to our hearts.

All through the New Testament Jesus taught the multitudes by telling them stories or parables to illustrate spiritual principles. He explained the unknown by using the known. Jesus said, "The kingdom of heaven is like a man who sowed good seed in his field..." "The kingdom of heaven is like a mustard seed..." "The kingdom of God is like treasure hidden in a field..." "The kingdom of God is like a net that was let down into the lake and caught all kinds of fish..." Likewise, Jesus continues to illustrate spiritual principles through modern day parables. He shows up in our lives every day, but we must turn aside and pay attention.

When Moses saw a burning bush in the desert that was not being consumed, he *turned aside*, stopped what he was doing, and went to investigate this amazing sight. "When the LORD saw that he *turned aside* to look, God called to him from the midst of the bush, and said, 'Moses, Moses!' And he said, 'Here I am'" (Exodus 3:4 NASB, emphasis added).

Ah, there's the key. Moses *turned aside*. God had his full attention. Could it be that we become so wrapped up in our daily activities and to-do lists that we don't take the time to *turn aside* when God speaks? I wonder how many burning bushes I've missed in my own backyard. I fear we have grown unaccustomed to listening, uninterested in what He has to say, or unbelieving that He will speak to us.

God created us to be in a relationship with Him. He tells us time and time again that we will be blessed when we listen to what He says and obey His commands. "Blessed are your eyes because they see, and your ears because they hear" (Matthew 13:16).

Does God still speak to us today? I'm absolutely sure He does. But don't take my word for it—take Jesus' word. He said, "I am the good shepherd...My sheep listen to my voice; I know them, and they follow me" (John 10:14,27). Since God continues to speak today, why do we have such difficulty recognizing His voice? Why don't we hear Him more often? Hearing God's voice should be part of the normal everyday experience for a child of God. It is God's *silence* that should give us reason for concern, for in times past, God's silence was a form of punishment for disobedience. Also, hearing God's voice is not only for the "super Christian," if there is such a thing. It is for the uneducated fisherman, the woman in the kitchen, the leprous outcast, the tax collector in a tree, and for you and me. I hope by the end of this book, recognizing God's voice will become a common occurrence in your life.

Author Ken Gire asks, "Should we even expect Him to speak in the everyday moments of our lives? Or should we be content with echoes, however eloquent, from the past? If God does still speak, perhaps some of those words are words for us. Perhaps He is offering us in the mid afternoons of our lives small slices of heaven to stave off the hunger—or maybe arouse it."[2]

I haven't heard God's audible voice, but He does speak to me on a regular basis. I've felt His nudge in the kitchen as I've mopped the linoleum floor, I've recognized His tug as I've pulled off the highway in an overheated car, I've sensed His peaceful wooing as I've struggled to weather tumultuous storms, I've heard echoes of His laughter as He's instructed me to learn from the children in my care, I've sensed His presence as I spent time meditating on the Scriptures.

I invite you to join me on a journey of learning to be a woman who listens to God. In the teaching style of Jesus, I'll share biblical principles intertwined with modern day parables from my own life. My hope and prayer is that you will begin to recognize God's presence in your own life and *become a woman who listens to God*.

Earth is crammed with heaven,
And every common bush afire with God,
But only he who sees, takes off his shoes.

ELIZABETH BARRETT BROWNING

ONE

God Speaks Through His Word

I REMEMBER WHEN MY SON, STEVEN, was four years old and playing in the backyard with one of the neighborhood kids. They were having an argument about who authored the Bible.

"The Bible was written by God," Steven said.

"No it wasn't," the other boy exclaimed. "It was just written by a bunch of men."

"You're wrong," Steven countered. "Those men just held the pen, but God told them what to write."

Back and forth the boys bantered. Of course, at four years old, the dueling theologians were simply repeating what they had heard from their parents. But their battle mimics the battle of faith that is waged for every person at one time or another. Is God who He says He is? Can He do what He says He can do? Are the words in the Bible God's Words or man's?

The most obvious way that God speaks today is through the Scriptures. The Bible tells us, "All Scripture is God-breathed and is useful for teaching, rebuking, correcting and training in righteousness, so that the man of God may be thoroughly equipped for every good work" (2 Timothy 3:16-17). Some translations render

"God-breathed" as "inspired." But the Greek word *theopneustos* is more than inspired, more than influenced, more then enlightened—it is actually "God breathed." Interestingly, when God created Adam, he was a lifeless form, a mere shell, until God breathed the breath of life into his nostrils and he became a living being. Likewise, our spirits are dead until God breathes life into our spirits through the life-giving Word. James tells us, "He chose to give us birth through the word of truth, that we might be a kind of first fruits of all he created" (James 1:18). Moses told the Israelites, "Man does not live by bread alone but by every word that comes from the mouth of the LORD" (Deuteronomy 8:3). Yes, God's Word gives us life!

The Bible tells us that the Scriptures *are alive*. John calls Scriptures "the Word of life" (1 John 1:1). Peter calls Scripture the "living and enduring word of God" (1 Peter 1:23). "For the word of God is living and active. Sharper than any double-edge sword, it penetrates even to dividing soul and spirit, joints and marrow; it judges the thoughts and attitudes of the heart" (Hebrews 4:12). No matter how long we live, no matter how many times we read through the Bible, God will continue to speak to us through the pages of His Word. His words are living and bring us life!

Peter reminds us, "Above all, you must understand that no prophecy of Scripture came about by the prophet's own interpretation. For prophecy never had its origin in the will of man, but men spoke from God as they were carried along by the Holy Spirit" (2 Peter 1:20-21). When the writers penned the words of the Bible, they were under the control of the Holy Spirit. David said, "The Spirit of the LORD spoke through me" (2 Samuel 23:2), and Jeremiah explained, "The LORD said to me…You must go to everyone I send you to and say whatever I command you" (Jeremiah 1:7).

The Hebrew word for "Bible" is *mikra*, which means "the calling out of God." He calls out to us from the pages and speaks to us through the words. The Bible is amazingly profound and yet simple enough for a child to understand. The more time we spend in the Scriptures, the more God will reveal the truths within.

One summer I went to Europe and visited many art museums. I recall strolling down the aisles of the Louvre in Paris, quickly glancing at first one masterpiece and then another. Finally, I decided to stop and look at one particular painting. I don't even remember which one it was. The more I looked at the painting, the more I began to see. It was dark on one side and grew lighter on the other. I noticed the expressions on the faces, the longing of a child, the pain of a man, the approaching cloud in the sky, the hues of the clothes, a bare foot, a torn robe, a clenched fist. A story began to unfold before my eyes, and it was as if I were beginning to see into the heart of the artist.

This reminded me of how some read the Bible—like perusing through an art gallery and never really stopping to see what the artist intended in the great masterpieces lining the majestic walls. Like walking briskly through an art gallery, we grab the Bible and read a few verses before running out the door in the morning or closing our eyes at night.

But God's Word is a masterpiece, and He speaks through every stroke of the writer's pen. Oh, the treasures stored on each page just waiting to be discovered! Paul prayed that God would give us the Spirit of wisdom and revelation, so that we may know Him better and so that the eyes of our hearts may be enlightened in order that we may know the hope to which He has called us, the riches of His glorious inheritance in the saints, and His incomparably great power for us who believe (Ephesians 1:17-19). I pray that the eyes of our hearts will be open to see God through the pages of the Bible and hear His voice in each and every word.

Seek Me with Your Whole Heart

God promised, "You will seek me and find me when you seek me with all your heart" (Jeremiah 29:13). This is more than a casual glance before heading off to work or to the carpool in the morning. It's more than a hit-and-run encounter with God. He desires to speak to us through the pages of our Bibles, and hearing Him requires meditating and seeking Him with our whole hearts.

Jesus told His followers, "If you abide in My Word, then you are truly disciples of Mine; and you shall know the truth, and the truth shall make you free" (John 8:31-32 NASB). *Abide* means to continue in, to tarry, to dwell, to remain. It is not reading the Scriptures for information, but for transformation. There are many scholars who have read the Bible for information but have never entered into a relationship with Jesus Christ. This reminds me of the difference between a woman who memorizes a menu at a restaurant and a woman who enjoys the food. Only one gets fed!

Let me ask you, who can describe a sunset more accurately— a blind person who has read all about sunsets (what causes the colors, the time of day they occur, the effect of clouds on the hues) or the person who had seen and experienced the vibrant oranges, blues, pinks, and purples painted across the sky as the sun creeps below the horizon and the rays play peek-a-boo behind the scattered clouds? I dare say the one who has experienced the sunset for herself. When we study God's Word and couple that with listening to His voice, we will come to know Him on a much more intimate level than a biblical scholar who has studied the words on the page but never taken the time to converse with the Author Himself.

Jesus told us that when we hold to His teaching, we will become His disciples. (See John 8:31.) One thing I've noticed through the years, a Bible that is falling apart usually belongs to a person who isn't!

Bride in the Box

Every little girl dreams of the day when she will become a beautiful bride. At four years old, I was no exception. It wasn't the dream of becoming a wife that captured my imagination, but merely the dream of the wedding day itself. I had visions of gliding down the red carpeted aisle of my hometown church, adorned in a white flowing satin-and-chiffon wedding gown that was studded with a million tiny pearls. My 12-foot lace veil would fill the aisle from side to side just like Julie Andrews' in *The Sound of Music,* and on my feet would be tiny satin slippers. In my hands I would carry a large bouquet of white roses mingled with a spray of delicate baby's breath. Who the groom would be was of very little consequence. This was clearly to be my show. On rainy days, I would wrap a towel around my head, a sheet around my small frame, and practice the wedding march down the long hallway of my parents' home. I could almost hear the trumpets and organ blast with my processional.

Apparently, one of my uncles understood the secret longings of four-year-old little girls, and he presented me with a two-foot-tall doll dressed in full bridal regalia. This was clearly the most beautiful doll I had ever seen. Along with her white wedding gown and veil, she had short cropped curly brown hair that felt as real as my own, soft plump pink skin, and movable eyelids lined with thick black lashes. Her eyes opened and closed with her changing positions so that when she lay down in her box, she resembled Sleeping Beauty. Her perfectly shaped lips were small and dainty, and her crystal blue eyes appeared strangely real.

But there was one problem with this delightful gift. Because she was so expensive, my mother wouldn't allow me to play with her.

"You'll have to wait until you are older," she stated. "She's too nice of a doll, and you might tear her gown. We'll just keep her in the box until you're big enough to know how to take care of her."

The bride doll remained in her box, safely stowed away in the bottom drawer of my dresser. Day after day I would slowly open the drawer and stare at the doll as she lay sleeping like a treasure in a safety deposit box. Sometimes I would remove the box lid and gently stroke her soft pink skin, but I knew "woe is me" if I ever took her out of the box and played with her.

Now that I am an adult, my thoughts have gone back to that special gift. After a time I forgot about the bride in the dresser drawer, and today I don't even remember what became of her. As a child, my relationship with the Lord was much like my relationship with that doll. God was someone who was to be revered and feared, but certainly not someone to be touched and enjoyed. I had the impression that God, like the doll, was to be kept in a box: a big brick building with a large steeple on top that was only to be opened on Sunday and special holidays. But He was certainly not someone who would talk to you, or even wanted to.

The Shorter Catechism, written by the Westminster Assembly in 1647, states, "The chief end of man is to glorify God and enjoy Him forever." Enjoy Him! That was such a blinding revelation to me when I heard it for the first time. It took me years to understand what it means or how to go about the business of "enjoying" the Lord. David understood what it meant to enjoy the Lord. He wrote, "In Thy presence is fulness of joy. In Thy right hand there are pleasures forever" (Psalm 16:11 NASB). "I delight in your decrees. I will not neglect your word...Direct me in the path of your commands, for there I find delight...I delight in your commands because I love them" (Psalm 119:16,35,47). David even danced before the Lord. (See 2 Samuel 6.)

First Timothy 6:17 says that God "richly supplies us with all things to *enjoy*" (NASB, emphasis added). Webster defines "enjoy" as "to take *pleasure* or *delight* in, to have the *use,* the *benefit* or *advantage* of." (Emphasis added.) Even though the bride doll was a precious gift to me, I didn't enjoy her, delight in her, or have the pleasure of interacting with her. Likewise, if I keep God's Word at bay, keep it in a box, or leave it on a shelf, I miss the enjoyment and the delight of entering into a relationship with Him and listening to His voice in the pages of Scripture.

After reflecting on the bride doll, I decided to no longer keep God or His Word in a box for safekeeping. I will sing with Him, talk with Him, take walks with Him, and, yes, even dance with Him. And I don't have to wait until I am big enough to take care of Him because He is big enough to take care of me!

Logos vs. Rhema

There are two Greek words that mean "word." *Logos* is the entire Word of God from Genesis through Revelation. It is the "revealed will of God, a direct revelation given by Christ, it is the message from the Lord, delivered with His authority effective by His power. Sometimes it is used as the sum of ✣✣ utterances."[1]

There is another Greek word that is translated "word"—*rhema*. As the *logos* is the entire Word of God, *rhema* is a particular passage of Scripture that God quickens to your spirit. As we store up the *logos* of God in our hearts, God will speak a personal *rhema* to our hearts. This may occur when you are reading the Bible or when the Holy Spirit brings a verse to mind that you have previously read. Let's say you are praying about a certain matter and asking God to give you direction through His Word. As you read the Bible, God may lead you to a certain verse or speak to you from the passages you are studying. I have never been one to recommend Bible roulette, closing my eyes, opening the Bible, and randomly pointing to a verse for my answer. However, I do believe that as we read the Bible, God will speak to our hearts.

For example, when I was praying about whether or not to be a part of Proverbs 31 Ministries and a radio cohost, I prayed for several weeks. God had spoken to me through a certain circumstance, which I will share a bit later, but then He confirmed His will through Scripture. I heard a sermon about Jesus turning the water to wine at the first miracle at the wedding of Cana. When the wedding party ran out of wine, Jesus' mother turned to the servants and said, "Whatever He [Jesus] says to you, do it" (John 2:5 NASB).

This was a *rhema* word from God to me. I knew God was telling me to "do it!" My husband was sitting in the same service, but he wasn't particularly moved by the passage. I, on the other hand, was about to jump out of my seat. Why? Because God had spoken directly to me! He had spoken to me through a particular circumstance, and now He was confirming my direction through His Word. I knew God was telling me to take the first steps of faith and follow the path He had laid out for me.

Ephesians 6:17 commands us to take up "the sword of the Spirit, which is the word of God." Guess which Greek word is used for "word"? *Rhema*—a particular word that the Holy Spirit brings to our remembrance. But remember, in order for the Holy Spirit to bring a *rhema* to our remembrance, the *logos* has to be deposited in our memory banks first.

There will be times when God impresses a certain word or words on our hearts, but we must be careful not to impose that word onto others. Let me give you this example from John Newton, ex-slave trader and author of the song "Amazing Grace." He wrote, "All true believers walk by the same rule and pay attention to the same things. The Word of God is their compass. The Lord Jesus is both their polar star and their sun of righteousness. Their hearts and faces are all set heavenward. They are one in Body. One Holy Spirit lives in them. Yet their experiences, based on these same principles, are far from identical...We must not make the experiences of others a rule binding us, nor make our experiences a rule for others."[2]

Newton warned us of the dangers of taking a word that God has for us personally and imposing it on the entire body of Christ.

God-Sense vs. Common Sense

Sitting in my backyard, I love to listen to the sounds of all God's critters: birds, crickets, frogs, katydids, woodpeckers, and, most of all, children. Framing our yard from every side, children's giggles, chatter, and raucous play are a symphony of stringed instruments and percussions alike. There's the rhythmic thumping of a basketball bouncing on concrete, the squealing of little girls being chased by boys, the skidding of bicycle tires on asphalt, the popping of a cap gun, declarations of "you're it," and contentions of "you cheated" all blending together in a symphony of youth. Of course, the orchestra would not be complete without the reprimands of parents breaking up fights and reminders to stubborn wills of house rules.

Rules, rules, rules. What a bother—especially when you are five years old. When I was five, I never understood why parents had to interfere and ruin the fun with rules. I eventually decided it was just part of their job description. Parents: Law enforcement officers who patrol the neighborhood, ruining all the fun for little girls and boys.

As a five-year-old tomboy, my favorite possession was a pink sparkly bicycle with a silver glittery banana seat and U-shaped handlebars. Streamers were attached to the ends of the handles and blew in the breeze as I pedaled around the neighborhood at breakneck speed. I could leave skid marks as long as any old boy, balance without holding onto the handlebars, and do wheelies with my front tire saluting the air. Oh, how I loved to ride around the racetrack (otherwise known as Pine Haven Drive) feeling the wind whip through my ash-blonde hair and brush past my bare chest. It was the "bare chest" part that was the problem.

"Sharon Ann Edwards," my mother would call from the front porch. "Get in the house this minute and put on a shirt!"

"I don't want to wear a shirt," I whined. "Stewart doesn't have to wear a shirt. Why do I?"

"Because you're a girl and because I said so. That's why."

My brother was five years my senior, and he often romped around without a shirt. As far as I could tell, there wasn't any difference between him and me. So why did people snicker when I rode past them bare-chested? I just didn't get it. Begrudgingly, I'd knock down my kickstand, stomp through the house, and pull on a T-shirt, mumbling all the way.

This was not a one-time incident, and my mother tired of making me dress like a girl, or, should I say, dress period. But then something amazing happened. I entered first grade. Suddenly things clicked and I noticed that boys and girls were indeed different. It all started with Isaac Thorp and his big blue eyes. Well, Mom never had to tell me to keep my shirt on again.

Rules—what a bother. Rules—what a comfort. Eventually, I learned that even if I didn't completely understand one of my parents' mandates, it would usually make sense later on. In the same way, I learned that if I didn't understand one of my heavenly Father's rules, it would usually make sense later on. God's principles are not randomly contrived to ruin our fun. They are meticulously thought out and created to protect His children. God is a lot smarter than we are. Have you noticed that? If I question Him and He answers, "Because I said so," well, that's good enough for me, and hopefully I'll figure the reason out later—but I may not. If I don't, I just need to remember that Father knows best.

Sometimes when we are reading God's Word, He may tell us to do something that may not make sense to us. He told Noah to build an ark when he had never seen rain before. He told Joshua to march around Jericho in silence for seven days and then let out a shout that would make the walls of the great city crumble. He gave the Israelites many dietary rules that modern science has come to discover are the healthiest ways to eat. He told the Jews to circumcise baby boys on the eighth day, and today doctors have discovered that our blood clotting factor is greatest on...the eighth day.

Early one morning, after Peter had spent an entire night fruitlessly fishing, Jesus told him to throw his nets back into the water. I love Peter's reply to this carpenter. "Master, we've worked hard all night and haven't caught anything. *But because you say so*, I will let down the nets" (Luke 5:5, emphasis added).

Because You said so...I can think of no better reason to listen and obey God's voice.

"When they had done so, they caught such a large number of fish that their nets began to break. So they signaled their partners in the other boat to come and help them, and they came and filled both boats so full that they began to sink" (Luke 5:6-7).

A Treasured Love Letter

Yes, God does speak to us through the pages of Scripture with guidelines for abundant life, but the Bible is so much more than a lists of do's and don'ts. It is a love letter from God's heart to ours.

It is one thing to approach the Bible as a scholar, but it is quite another to savor the words as an intimate love letter written to you—the beloved. Ken Gire, in his book *The Reflective Life*, gives the example of Ken Burns, who produced a series on the Civil War for PBS. His work began by sifting through old photographs, maps, diaries, historical records, letters, and memoirs. In his search, he stumbled across a letter that personified what he wanted to accomplish with the documentary. His desire was to do more than present the facts. History books can do that. He wanted to present the heart—the personal side of the war.

July 14, 1861
Camp Clark, Washington
My very dear Sarah:

The indications are very strong that we shall move in a few days—perhaps tomorrow. Lest I should not be able to write again, I feel impelled to write a few lines that may fall under your eye when I shall be no more...

I have no misgivings about, or lack of confidence in the strong cause in which I am engaged, and my courage does not halt or falter. I know how strongly American Civilization now leans on the triumph of the Government, and how great a debt we owe to those who went before us through the blood and suffering of the Revolution. And I am willing—perfectly willing—to lay down all my joys in this life, to help maintain this Government, and to pay that debt...

Sarah, my love for you is deathless. It seems to bind me with mighty cables that nothing but Omnipotence could break, and yet my love of Country comes over me like a strong wind and bears me unresistibly on with all these chains to the battlefield.

The memories of the blissful moments I have spent with you come creeping over me, and I feel most gratified to God and to you that I have enjoyed them so long. And hard it is for me to give them up and turn to ashes the hopes of future years when, God willing, we might have lived and loved together, and seen our sons grown up to honorable manhood around us. I have, I know, but few and small claims upon Divine Providence, but something whispers to me—perhaps it is the wafted prayer of my little Edgar, that I shall return to my loved one unharmed. If I do not, my dear Sarah, never forget how much I love you, and when my last breath escapes me on the battlefield, it will whisper your name. Forgive my many faults and the many pains I have caused you. How thoughtless and foolish I often have been! How gladly I would wash out with my tears every little spot upon your happiness...

But, O Sarah! If the dead can come back to this earth and flit unseen around those they loved, I shall always be near you; in the gladdest days and in the darkest nights...always, always, and if there be a soft breeze upon your cheek, it shall be my breath, as the cool air fans your throbbing temples, it shall be my spirit passing by. Sarah do not mourn me dead; think I am gone and wait for thee, for we shall meet again...[3]

Sullivan Ballou died at the first battle of Bull Run.

Gire concluded, "This is what the war meant to so many people on both sides. Fathers who would not be coming home. Or sons. Families that would never be the same again. Wives who would be left to raise a family alone, plant crops alone, face an uncertain future alone. So he would never forget the reason why he was making the documentary, Burns folded the letter and kept it in his shirt pocket during the entire time he was working on the film."[4]

We can approach Ballou's letter as a historian or a linguist, but if we do, we miss the point. The same is true with the Bible. We can study the Bible from a historical point of view, from a Hebrew and Greek perspective, or even as a great literary work. But if we do, we will miss the point. The Bible is first and foremost a love letter in which God desires to speak to our hearts, move our spirits, and nourish our souls. And when we read John 14–17, Jesus' final words seem to strike an amazing resemblance to Ballou's letter to Sarah. His last breath escaped Him on the battlefield of the cross with your name, and that soft breeze upon your cheek is the Holy Spirit passing by.

Time Well Spent

Sometimes you may read the Bible and feel that God is not speaking to you through what you have read. That's okay. During times like these think of it as though you are storing up grain for the winter or ammunition for the battle. Reading God's Word is never a waste of time—His Word will not return void.

> "'For my thoughts are not your thoughts, neither are your ways my ways,' declares the LORD. "As the heavens are higher than the earth, so are my ways higher than your ways and my thoughts than your thoughts. As the rain and the snow come down from heaven, and do not return to it without watering the earth and making it bud and flourish, so that it yields seed for the sower and bread for the eater, so is my word that goes out from my mouth: *It will not return to me empty, but will accomplish what I desire and achieve the purpose for which I sent it*" (Isaiah 55:8-11, emphasis added).

Oh dear friend, I pray that "out of his glorious riches he may strengthen you with power through his Spirit in your inner being, so that Christ may dwell in your hearts through faith. And I pray that you, being rooted and established in love, may have power, together with all the saints, to grasp how wide and long and high and deep is the love of Christ, and to know this love that surpasses knowledge—that you may be filled to the measure of all the fullness of God" (Ephesians 3:15-19). The more time we spend in God's Word, the more in tune we will be to His voice.

Whether burning bush or gentle whisper, Lord, I want to hear you.

Which Character Will You Play?

One Saturday night, my family hunkered down on the den sofa with an oversized bowl of popcorn, tall glasses of soda, and an action-packed video: *Raiders of the Lost Ark,* starring Harrison Ford. We were ready to be entertained by suspense, intrigue, and a touch of romance. Like any good movie, there were three principal characters: the good guy, the bad guy, and the damsel in distress. The good guy, Dr. Indiana Jones, who was a professor of archeology, obtainer of rare antiquities, and student of the world-renowned Dr. Ravenwood of the University of Chicago, quickly charmed us. The bad guy, a waxy-faced Nazi with a sinister grin and breathy laugh, who was always accompanied by an entourage of brutal, salivating, gargantuan henchmen, quickly appalled us. And then there was the damsel in distress—the not-so-fair Marian, daughter of the now deceased Dr. Ravenwood and sole proprietor of a drinking establishment in the snowy mountains of Nepal.

In the opening scene, Dr. Jones is pulled from teaching his archeology class to meet with two agents from U.S. Army Intelligence. It seems that Hitler is obsessed with religion and the occult and is on a mission to find the whereabouts of the Ark of the Covenant, which has been missing since Solomon's temple was destroyed in 586 B.C. Obviously, the government officials missed a few days in Sunday school, so Dr. Jones fills them in on the significance of this rare treasure. The Ark contains the Ten Commandments and symbolizes the presence of God.

The government officials explain they have intercepted a German communication that reveals the Nazis are searching for the Ark of the Covenant in Cairo, but in order to determine its exact location, they need a map that is engraved on a gold medallion, once owned by Dr. Ravenwood. Dr. Jones' mission, should he choose to accept it, is to locate the medallion, uncover the Ark of the Covenant, and bring it safely back to the United States.

Professor Jones, with the gleam of adventure in his eyes, whisks off his bow tie and wire-rimmed glasses and dons his suede Indiana Jones hat, leather whip, and trusty pistol. Off he goes to Nepal to find Marian and, hopefully, the medallion (which she has been wearing around her neck for years). Unfortunately for Marian, the waxy-faced Nazi also realizes that she is the key to finding the map, and he pays her a little visit just before Indiana Jones arrives. In adventure film fashion, a fight ensues, a fire breaks out, and the damsel's life is in peril. Just before the blazing walls come crashing down, the spy notices the gold medallion engulfed in flames and hanging from a pole. Without considering the consequences, he grabs the metal disk from the flames, only to quickly drop it from his hot little hand, but not before it leaves a lasting impression. One side of the map is forever burned into his palm. Of course, Indiana Jones comes to the rescue. The music soars, the hero cracks his whip, saves the damsel in distress, and recovers the medallion.

The Germans, thinking they have the map in the palm of their hand (actually the palm of Mr. Waxy-Face's hand), start to dig. But what Professor Jones realizes is that the map is actually on the front and back of the medallion. The Germans have only half of the map and thus are digging in the wrong place.

Now I have to tell you, this was supposed to be an evening of mindless entertainment, but God spoke to me in a big way. He used this movie to teach me about searching for His presence, hearing His voice, and how different people go about it. Many people would like to have the presence of God in their camp. And just as in the movie, we can potentially play one of three roles.

Some people are like the damsel, who had been wearing the treasure map around her neck for years without having any idea as to what it was. She only wore it because her beloved father had given it to her as a gift. Likewise, there are those who wear a cross around their neck, but they don't truly understand the significance of the gift of sacrifice and salvation from their heavenly Father. There are others who have a dusty Bible on a crowded bookshelf or displayed on a living room coffee table, but they don't realize that it contains God's Words to them. They don't understand that the Bible is the map to experiencing God's presence and hearing His voice in their daily lives.

Some are like the bad guy with only one side of the medallion burned into the palm of his hand. They have heard parts of Scripture, read a few verses here and there, or visited a church on holy days such as Easter or Christmas. They are searching for the hidden treasure of life, but because they don't understand the whole truth of God, they are digging in the wrong place.

Finally, some are like the heroic Dr. Jones, who possessed the whole map and knew exactly where to search for the treasure above all treasure—the Ark of the Covenant—the presence of God. Oh, the joy that comes from following God's map...not just parts of it...but all of it. God has not left us alone to figure out this thing called life on our own. He speaks to us through the pages of the Bible to tell us great and mighty things we do not know (Jeremiah 33:3 NASB).

The movie was over. My popcorn bowl was empty, but my heart was full. As the credits rolled across the screen, God seemed to say, "There are three principal roles. Which character will you play?"

TWO

God Speaks Through the Holy Spirit

WHILE GOD SPEAKS THROUGH THE BIBLE, it is the Holy Spirit who opens our eyes to see and ears to hear. It is virtually impossible to separate the work of the Holy Spirit and the work of the Word of God, for they work in tandem to help us become women who listen to God. Just as a seed cannot germinate and grow in the earth without water, the seeds of Scripture cannot germinate and grow in our hearts without the Spirit. Just as water seeps into the soil and penetrates the seed's protective shell, the Holy Spirit seeps through the soul and penetrates the heart to cause spiritual growth and enlightenment. "Flesh gives birth to flesh, but Spirit gives birth to spirit," Jesus explained (John 3:6). The Holy Spirit is called "the Spirit of truth" (John 14:17), and He reveals truth on the pages of Scripture.

Over the centuries much mystery has surrounded the person of the Holy Spirit. In times past He's been referred to as the "Holy Ghost," which conjures for us visions of spirits or ghosts. Various denominations place differing emphasis on the Holy Sprit, who He is, and what role He plays in a believer's life. Some denominations, in an attempt to avoid the confusion, have ignored the person and work of the Spirit altogether. The Holy Spirit is part of the Trinity—God the Father, God the Son, and God the Holy Spirit. Admittedly, it is easier to conceptualize the idea of a father and a son. However, Jesus clearly taught that the Holy Spirit was a person who would be active in the lives of believers once He had ascended to heaven. Where does that leave those who ignore Him? I'm not sure, but I am sure I don't want to be one to find out!

In the Old Testament, the Holy Spirit filled men and women for a certain amount of time, in order to accomplish a particular task. He filled Moses with the Holy Spirit and gave him wisdom to appoint judges (Numbers 11:16-17). God appointed Bezalel and Oholiab to work with silver and gold when building the tabernacle and then filled them with the Holy Spirit, who taught them how (Exodus 31:1-6). God filled Gideon with the Holy Spirit and gave him the courage to lead the Israelites into battle (Judges 6:34). The writer of the book of Judges penned, "Then the Spirit of the LORD came upon Gideon." The actual Hebrew words for "came upon" mean the Spirit "clothed Gideon with Himself."

In the New Testament, we find a difference in the permanence of the Holy Spirit into a person's life. In the Old Testament, the Holy Spirit was given for a season of time to accomplish a specific task. God withdrew the Holy Spirit from a person once their task was complete or if they disobeyed His command. This is precisely what happened to Saul when he sinned against God (1 Samuel 16:14). In the New Testament, Jesus promised all believers that the Holy Spirit, the Counselor, the Comforter (KJV), would come to abide in us and never leave or forsake us (John 14:16).

Once someone accepts Jesus as his or her personal Savior, the Holy Spirit comes and takes up residence in that person. "Don't you know that you yourselves are God's temple and that God's Spirit lives in you?" Paul wrote (1 Corinthians 3:16). Because the Holy Spirit abides in each believer, we should expect Him to speak to us on a regular basis. But each time we resist the Spirit (Acts 7:51), grieve the Spirit (Ephesians 4:30), or quench the Spirit

(1 Thessalonians 5:19 NASB), we throw a cup of water onto the flame. The Holy Spirit won't leave us, but His power in our lives may be reduced to a smoldering ember if we refuse to listen.

He Convicts

The Holy Spirit does speak to non-believers. However, He primarily speaks to convict them of sin and the need to repent, and the need to come to saving faith in Jesus Christ. The Holy Spirit speaks to believers to convict us of sin as well. Just like an unbeliever, we have the choice to heed His warnings or turn a deaf ear.

In my own life, when the Holy Spirit speaks to me concerning a particular sin, it is almost as if He is screaming at me to stop and think about what I'm getting ready to do or the potential consequences of my unholy actions. If I ignore His promptings, the next time His voice isn't quite as loud. Eventually, if I continue to choose to ignore the Holy Spirit's voice, I may not hear His voice at all. Paul wrote to the Thessalonians, "Do not put out the Holy Spirit's fire" (1 Thessalonians 5:19). Another version says, "Do not quench the Spirit" (NASB). Each time we ignore Him, we diminish our ability to hear His voice.

Let's say I turn the television to a program that I know God would not want me to watch. I feel the Holy Spirit's conviction and sense Him speaking to me to turn the television off and not fill my mind with visions and words that are unpleasing to God. If I ignore the Holy Spirit and watch the program, it is as though I develop "spiritual wax buildup" and the next time the Holy Spirit speaks, His voice is not quite as clear. I believe with all my heart that turning a deaf ear to the Holy Spirit's conviction in our lives will lead to a serious case of hearing loss. The only solution is repentance—which is more than saying, "I'm sorry," but turning and going in the opposite direction.

The Melting Pot

Going to an amusement park has never been very amusing to me. Climbing a mountainous rickety wooden track while sitting in a two-seater metal box with a flimsy bar across my lap for safety and then being plunged a hundred feet to the ground, expecting to meet Jesus at any moment, is not my idea of relaxation. Being herded through a roped maze and standing in line for hours to endure a ride that lasts 90 seconds is definitely not entertaining. Spinning in circles makes me nauseous.

Why then, you ask, would I subject myself to such spinning, plunging, gyrating, pendulating, and lunging into oblivion? The answer's easy. I love my family. I've endured roller coasters with my son, been turned upside down and spun in a corkscrew with my niece, and had my insides scrambled with my nephews. All to see their smiles and make memories I'll never forget.

Amusement parks are the great melting pots of America. On one occasion while I was standing in a line waiting to become airborne on the death defying "Gauntlet," I was struck by the sideshow of humanity surrounding me. A 14-year-old girl in minuscule cut-off shorts and a bikini bathing suit top, with her body covered in baby oil and glitter was standing next to a pot-bellied motorcyclist with a skull and crossbones tattooed on his left shoulder, a ring through his pierced nose, and stringy blond hair hanging down his furry bare back. There was a group of snaggletoothed illiterates spitting tobacco juice and watching it sizzle on the 101-degree asphalt.

As I stood in disgust among this melting pot of humanity, queasy from the sights and smells of unwashed bodies and greasy hair, the Holy Spirit began to convict my prideful heart. *Yes, you are clean and polished, standing here with manicured nails, pressed linen shorts, and a designer T-shirt. Your children reflect your lifestyle choices and upbringing. But I didn't come just for the lovely, neatly groomed, and freshly scented of society. I came for the foul-smelling shepherd, leprous outcast, and uneducated fisherman. I came for the glitter-covered girl, the nose-pierced gang member, and the snaggletoothed illiterate. These are all My sheep. I love each and every one of them just as much as I love you. They are all My children.*

The veil was lifted from my eyes, and my disgust turned to compassion. These were my brothers and sisters—or at least they could be. Jesus loved them just as much as He loved me. He welcomed them and gave His life for them—just as He had for me.

I began to use my time in line to pray. *Lord, whatever pain that young teen has experienced to cause her to dress so risqué̃ly and draw attention to herself, heal those hurts. Draw her to Yourself and help her to come to know You as her loving Father. May the man with the pierced nose one day have his heart pierced by the conviction of Your great love and sacrifice for him. May the snaggletoothed illiterate be filled with the knowledge of Jesus Christ and Your will in all spiritual wisdom and understanding.*

My heart was filled with love for this merry band, and I was just about to call us all together for a big group hug when I realized it was time for my group to be loaded in our metal seat and strapped in place. Once again I was spun around at breakneck speed, turned on my head, and jerked to a sudden stop from 60 miles per hour. The rides were exciting, but not nearly as exciting as the convicting conversation I had with the Holy Spirit while in line.

He Comforts

Have you ever had times in your life when you needed a holy hug? I know I have. There have been days when nothing else would do but for Jesus to wrap His loving arms around me, remind me of His precious promises, and calm all my fears. "Peace I leave with you; my peace I give to you. I do not give to you as the world gives. Do not let your hearts be troubled and do not be afraid" (John 14:27). "In this world you will have trouble," Jesus warned. "But take heart! I have overcome the world" (John 16:33).

For about ten years, I struggled with infertility and then the loss of a child. During that time, there were many days when there were no words to comfort me. More than my husband, more than my friends, more than my extended family, I needed my heavenly Comforter.

The Holy Spirit speaks words to our spirits to give us comfort, peace, and reassurance. Sometimes outsiders may not understand how we can have such peace in our lives when there is much turmoil, but the peace the Holy Spirit gives is supernatural—it is the peace that passes all understanding.

One Sunday morning I was teaching a group of four-year-old children the story of Jesus calming the storm on the Sea of Galilee. I painted a rather bleak picture of the 12 disciples and their teacher in a tiny fishing boat trapped in the storm: huge waves splashing over the boat, giant flashes of lightning, reverberating claps of thunder, the up and down and up and down rolling of the boat in the sea. Finally I asked, "If you were caught in a storm like this in a tiny boat, would you be afraid?"

Then one little girl shrugged her shoulders and replied, "Not if Jesus was in the boat with me."

Ah, she understood peace. Jesus is always in the boat with us, and He gives us peace that passes all understanding, peace that makes no earthy sense but is truly heaven sent. This is the comfort that only the Holy Spirit can give.

Messenger from Heaven

My new friend Katie lay in her bed trying not to think about the pain in her abdomen. For years she had taken care of many patients as she nursed the sick back to health. But now *she* was the patient. Just four weeks had passed since her doctor said words that kept echoing in her mind.

"Katie, it isn't an ulcer, like we originally thought. It's cancer—pancreatic cancer. And it has already spread to your liver and your lungs."

"How long do I have?" she questioned.

"I'd say about three to six months," he replied.

Three to six months. She replayed her past 50 years on the stage of her mind. Her thoughts were filled with frantic questions. "How did this happen? What went wrong? How did I get to this point?"

Katie had accepted Jesus as her Savior when she was a young child. But that seemed a lifetime ago, and in a way it was. Now her thoughts were filled with shame, regret, and guilt. The verses of the woman at the well came to mind. Jesus spoke to the Samaritan woman and said, "Woman, where is your husband?"

She answered and said, "I have no husband."

Jesus replied, "You have well said, 'I have no husband,' for you have had five husbands and the one who you now have is not your husband." (See John 4:16-17.)

"Lord, You know all that I've done," Katie prayed. "How I've fallen away from following You. I've been married twice, and the man I'm living with now is not my husband. Is that why this is happening to me? Am I being punished? People have told me that You still love me, but I feel so alone. Have You left me too, like all the other men in my life?"

Katie reached for her Bible, and it fell open to Luke 3 where John was baptizing Jesus. "And the Holy Spirit descended upon Him in bodily form like a dove, and a voice came out of heaven saying. 'Thou art my beloved Son, in Thee I am well pleased'" (Luke 3:22 NASB).

Tears ran down Katie's dry cheeks like streams in the desert. "Where are You, Lord? Please don't desert me."

Katie turned her head to look out at the sun glistening over the tranquil lake in her backyard. Suddenly, as though he emerged from the pages of Luke 3, a dove fluttered to her windowsill and perched on its ledge.

Katie hugged her Bible to her chest as she and the dove locked eyes. He seemed to say, "Yes, Katie. I do love you. You may have strayed away from the path that I had marked out for you, but that hasn't changed My love. I never left you, and I'll stay right here by your side until the day I come to take you home."

The dove stayed on the windowsill for quite some time, and Katie thanked the Lord for sending His messenger like the one from long ago. And indescribable warmth fell over her body as she realized that God did indeed still love her.

Three months later, that dove came again to my friend Katie. Only this time, when he soared back toward heaven, Katie's spirit went with him.

He Counsels

During Jesus' last supper discourse, He reassured the disciples that He would not leave them as orphans. "I will ask the Father, and he will give you another Counselor to be with you forever—the Spirit of truth" (John 14:16-17). The Greek word here for "counselor," which is also translated *Helper* (NASB) and *Comforter* (KJV), is *parakletos* and means a "person summoned to one's aid."[1] Originally it was a term used in a court of justice to denote a legal assistant, counsel for the defense, an advocate; then, generally, one who pleads another's cause, an intercessor, an advocate.[2]

I love the image of being in a court of law because I have come to see Satan as the "accuser of our brethren" (Revelation 12:10 NASB). He points his gnarly finger in our faces and says things like, "You aren't a very good Christian," "Jesus doesn't really love you," "You were a mistake when you were born," "You've really blown it this time," "I don't see much fruit in your life," "You're a pitiful excuse as a wife, as a mother, as a child of God," and so on. Now tell me, have you ever heard any of those statements before? Perhaps you've always assumed these were your own musings. That's exactly what Satan would have you believe. However, I believe those accusatory statements are words from Satan that he whispers in our ears. They sound like us, they feel like us, but they're from the accuser himself. It is always amazing to me that while I might have trouble hearing God's voice, Satan's usually comes through loud and clear.

On the other hand, the Holy Spirit is our counselor, our attorney, the one who comes alongside us and repeats, "Not guilty! Not guilty! Not guilty!" He says, "You, My child, have been set free! Your debt has been paid in full."

The Redemption Center

If I think about it long enough, I can almost taste the sickly sweet glue on the tip of my tongue. Yes, the childhood ritual of licking and sticking S&H Green Stamps into books is forever glued in my memory's scrapbook.

When I was a little girl, my mother did her grocery shopping at White's Supermarket on the corner of Tarboro Street and Pearl. Oh sure, there were other grocery stores around, but White's gave out S&H Green Stamps with every purchase. On shopping days, I watched as the cashier rang up my mom's purchases, pulling a lever with each entry. My mom's eyes lit up every time she heard the cha-ching, knowing that meant more stamps. When the total tallied, the cash register spit out a stream of stamps, both large and small. We never put the stamps in books right away. Mom stuffed them in a bag and waited until we could make a whole day of it.

About every six months, Mom pulled a brown paper grocery bag swollen with S&H Green Stamps down from a shelf. She spilled its contents on a table and announced, "Okay, Sharon, it's time to paste the stamps."

For hours it was lick, stick, lick, stick, lick, stick. Large stamps represented dollars spent and only three filled a page. Small stamps represented cents spent and 30 filled a page. I liked doing the dollars.

After six months of collecting stamps and six hours of pasting them in the books, my mom and I excitedly drove down to the S&H Green Stamp Redemption Center. With arms heavy laden, we plopped our day's work on the clerk's desk.

"Whatcha goina get?" I'd ask as we strolled up and down the aisles of housewares.

"I don't know, honey," my mom would reply. "But it'll be something good."

After much consternation, Mom would decide on a treasure such as an electric can opener, or a steam iron, or a shiny set of stainless steel mixing bowls. Oh, it was always exciting to make a trip to the S&H Green Stamp Redemption Center and trade in our stamps for a special prize.

Have you ever noticed there are some "Christianese" words we repeat often but have difficulty explaining? I think "redemption" is one of those words. But even as a child, because of my visits to the S&H trading store, I understood "redemption." To me, it meant to trade something in for something else, to take my stamps and trade them in (redeem them) for a prize—for something valuable.

Jesus Christ traded in His life to redeem mine. Listen to what these two passages have to say:

> Christ *redeemed* us from the curse of the law by becoming a curse for us, for it is written: "Cursed is everyone who is hung on a tree." He *redeemed* us in order that the blessing given to Abraham might come to the Gentiles through Christ Jesus, so that by faith we might receive the *promise of the Spirit* (Galatians 3:13-14, emphasis added).

> For you know that it was not with perishable things such as silver or gold that you were *redeemed* from the empty way of life handed down to you from your forefathers, but with the precious blood of Christ, a lamb without blemish or defect (1 Peter 1:18-19, emphasis added).

To Jesus, I was a prize—a treasure. But that's not all. He's made it possible for me to do a little bit of trading as well. I've traded in confusion for the mind of Christ, filthy rags for a robe of righteousness, bondage for freedom, bitterness for forgiveness, darkness for light, condemnation for acceptance, spiritual poverty for abundance, and the list goes on and on. There are gifts for this life and beyond. He even gave me (and you) the Holy Spirit as a down payment. What an abundance of treasures—much more valuable than an electric can opener or a set of mixing bowls.

As far as I know, there are no longer S&H Green Stamp Redemption Centers. But as long as there are sinners who need to be redeemed, there will always be a Savior who's anxious to make the trade.

He Clarifies

In 1 Corinthians chapter 2, Paul explains the role of the Holy Spirit in helping us hear and understand God's voice:

> We speak of God's secret wisdom, a wisdom that has been hidden and that God destined for our glory before time began. None of the rulers of this age understood it, for if they had, they would not have crucified the Lord of glory. However, as it is written: "No eye has seen, no ear has heard, no mind has conceived what God has prepared for those who love him"—but God has revealed it to us by his Spirit (1 Corinthians 2:7-10).

He goes on to say:

> We have not received the spirit of the world but the Spirit who is from God, that we may understand what God has freely given us. This is what we speak, not in words taught us by human wisdom, but in words taught by the Spirit, expressing spiritual truths in spiritual words. The man without the Spirit does not accept the things that come from the Spirit of God, for they are foolishness to him, and he cannot understand them, because they are spiritually discerned (verses12-14).

In other words, a man or woman without the Holy Spirit can't even begin to understand the deep truths of Scripture.

What has been so exciting to me over the years is how the Holy Spirit brings out various and deeper truths of Scripture the more time I spend in God's Word. He opens my heart to see new and amazing truths in verses I've read time and time again. So many times I've read a verse and thought, *Where did that come from? I have read that passage a hundred times and never seen that before!* The Holy Spirit speaks to us when we read the Word, and He expands and enriches our understanding of the Scriptures, God's character, and God's ways. When Jesus asked Peter, "Who do you say I am?" Peter answered, "You are the Christ, the Son of the living God." Jesus replied, "Blessed are you, Simon son of Jonah, for this was not revealed to you by man, but by my Father in heaven" (Matthew 16:15-17). Peter did not figure this out by himself. God revealed it to him.

We can always be certain God will not speak to us anything that is contradictory to His written Word. However, as we go through our day, He will, through the Holy Spirit, remind us of the words we have read and give us illustration after illustration to help us understand and apply those truths to our lives. I find myself saying to Him, "Oh, this is what You meant in the verses I read today," or "Now I understand what You meant by such and such." As I keep my heart in tune to hearing His voice, the Holy Spirit reminds me of certain passages throughout the day.

The Holy Spirit is the person who takes God's Word that we have stored in our hearts and brings it to remembrance. Jesus said, "The Holy Spirit will teach you all things and will remind you of everything I have said to you" (John 14:26). The Holy Spirit teaches us about God's character, His purposes, His ways, His nature, and His plans.

A few years ago, a phenomenon swept the country called "Magic Eye." These were colorful pictures that had a hidden picture within the picture. The way you discovered the hidden image was to hold the picture a certain distance from your face and then stare until your eyes went a bit out of focus. When you did it just right, another three-dimensional picture would pop into view. At least that's how it was supposed to work. However, I rarely if ever could get my eyes to find the hidden picture. I noticed that children seemed to be able to do it right away! I heard them shouting, "I see it! I see it!" while I sat cross-eyed, wondering what was wrong with my brain.

This reminds me of the process of reading Scripture. As I read, I pray that the Holy Spirit will reveal the "hidden picture." Then as He works to clarify God's Word, I begin to shout, "I see it! I see it!"

Confidence to Bank On

Do you think God has a sense of humor? Of course He does. Have you ever seen a baboon's red bottom or a gigantic hippopotamus's tail? Who else could have thought of such things had they not had a great sense of humor?

When God speaks to me, many times it causes a chuckle, if not from me, then from the people who are watching. I prefer it to be from me, but as God would have it, most of the time I do not get to choose. Let me share one particular incident with you.

As a teenager, I was never a particularly confident person, but I did learn how to act as though I were, even if I wasn't. When I went off to college to major in dental hygiene, the instructors taught us, "Now girls, when the patients come to the clinic for their cleaning appointments, you must act confident. You must act like you know what you are doing, even if you don't. If you act nervous, it will make the patients nervous."

For the first semester, I didn't have to worry about appearing confident because we just worked on a mannequin, whose name was Dexter. Dexter had a crank on the top of his head that we pulled when we wanted him to open his mouth and a rubber tongue that we safety pinned to his cheek when it got in the way. We all loved Dexter.

But the next semester the real patients came to the clinic. I found that real people were different from my friend Dexter. They did not have levers on the tops of their heads, and I could not fold up their tongue or pin it to their cheeks when it got in the way. And as uncomfortable as I was, it was part of my job to make these real people feel comfortable.

I made it through dental hygiene school, and the art of acting confident, even when I wasn't, proved very useful on several occasions in my adult life.

My husband, Steve, and I got married while we were still in college, and we had little funds for a honeymoon. With yard sale money, we took a quick trip to the Outer Banks of North Carolina, just three hours from my hometown. On our seventh anniversary, we decided to finally take that honeymoon trip, a cruise in the Bahamas. It was my job to make most of the travel preparations, which included purchasing traveler's checks from the bank. I had never used traveler's checks and didn't really know what to do. I didn't even know what a traveler's check looked like.

At this point, my "act confident even if you don't know what you are doing" training kicked in. I walked in the bank, and confidently, as though I had done this a million times, announced to the teller, "Excuse me, I would like to buy some traveler's checks."

Without looking up she asked, "What denomination?"

I thought that was a strange question, but answered, "Presbyterian. We go to a Presbyterian church."

The teller looked up, the corners of her lips curling into a sardonic grin as she said, "No, honey. I mean, do you want your checks in tens, twenties, or fifties?"

My confidence level plummeted and hovered somewhere below zero. I felt myself shrinking before the teller's very eyes as she enlightened me on a new word for the day. As I tried to find my voice, I squeaked, "Twenties will be fine." As she prepared the traveler's checks, I tried to remember Bible verses about money changers. I did not like this woman.

I got my traveler's checks, in denominations of $20, and crawled out of that bank, never to return. I'm sure she still tells that story at office parties and family reunions, and she will probably tell it to her grandchildren. I left not feeling very confident. This time the strategy had not worked.

I got in the car and bowed by head (actually, it was already bowed). Then the Lord reminded me of a few verses I had been studying but not quite understanding. "I put no confidence in the flesh," Paul said (Philippians 3:3). Lord, is this what You mean? *Yes, my child,* He seemed to say. *This is what you do most of the time. You depend on yourself to do and to be and to act. Sometimes your failures are comical, but sometimes they are not. Learn who you are in Christ, what you have in Christ, and where you are in Christ. Depend on Me and not on your weak self.*

I left the bank, totally humiliated in one sense but totally confident in another. "I am confident of this very thing, that He who began a good work in you will perfect it until the day of Christ Jesus" (Philippians 1:6 NASB). Now that's real confidence, and you can take that to the bank!

"The Bible is, first and foremost, a *love letter.* The words in that letter are like seeds that fall into the soil of our heart. With enough skill we can precisely measure the seeds, weigh them, and study them. No amount of skill, though, can bring the seeds to life. Only the Holy Spirit can do that. This is true of any word from God that lands in our heart—whether it's a word voiced through the Scriptures or through nature or through the circumstances of our lives. Each and every word that comes to us will lie dormant in the soil unless the Spirit gives it life.

"And there it will wait...quiet and still...for the rain."[3]

THREE

God Speaks Through Prayer

My HUSBAND, STEVE, GRADUATED from dental school in 1981. For the first two years, I was his only employee: his dental hygienist, dental assistant, receptionist, insurance clerk. On the days I was not helping him, I worked for another dentist in town. I was so exhausted most of the time that our joke became, "Sharon works six days a week and cries on the seventh."

One thing that amazed me, in starting a new practice, was all the emergency phone calls Steve received on nights and weekends. I usually answered the phone, and asked the caller several questions, one of which was, "Mrs. Jones, how long have you been having this problem?" Invariably the patient would say, "three days," "two weeks," "a month." I always thought, "So why did you wait until Saturday to call?" Of course, being the sweet person that I am, I never said that.

One night the phone rang at about 2:00 A.M. I groggily picked up the phone and managed a weak, "Hello?"

"Hello," the woman on the other end stated. "My son is having a terrible toothache. Is the doctor in?"

Where did she think he would be other than "in" at 2:00 in the morning? "Yes, ma'am, he is. How long has this tooth been bothering your son?"

"Oh, I'd say for about two weeks," she answered.

So why did you wait until now to call...I thought, not said, of course. I spoke with this mother for a few more minutes. Something about this call signaled a red flag in my mind. Then I asked, "Ma'am, how old is your son?"

She answered, "Twenty-seven. My son is 27 years old."

I was so shocked I quickly sat up in the bed, accidentally jerking the phone cord out of the wall and disconnecting the caller. She did not call back. I had envisioned a distraught mother with a crying five-year-old. But 27? Oh, my.

I laid back down complaining and grumbling. "Lord, why is it that people won't go to the doctor regularly but only want help on demand when they have an emergency?"

When I grew quiet enough to listen, I heard God's still, small voice whisper, "Now you know how I feel."

God speaks through His Word, through the Holy Spirit, and He speaks through prayer. Before we delve into the subject of prayer, I think we need to define exactly what prayer is and what prayer is not. Prayer is communion and communication with God. For us, as God's children, prayer includes praising God for who He is, thanking God for what He does, confessing our sin, asking for forgiveness, and petitioning God for our requests. There is also another key element to prayer—*listening for God's response.* Sometimes we tend to treat God like a celestial Santa Claus and sit down to pray with a wish list. But communion with God is much more than airing a wish list. Prayer is sitting at the feet of God with the attitude of the seraphim who cried, "holy, holy, holy is the LORD Almighty" (Isaiah 6:3). It is coming as a child communing with our heavenly Father. It is pressing our ear to the heart of God and listening to His desires.

One thing that makes the New Testament distinctively different from the Old Testament is that Jehovah God, the creator of the universe and all it contains, invites us to call Him *daddy*. It is the name of God that Jesus referred to more than any other. When the disciples asked Jesus to teach them how to pray, He said:

> When you pray, go into your room, close the door and pray to your *Father,* who is unseen. Then your *Father,* who sees what is done in secret, will reward you. And when you pray, do not keep on babbling like pagans, for they think they will be heard because of their many words. Do not be like them, for your *Father* knows what you need before you ask him. This then is how you should pray: "Our *Father* in heaven, hallowed be your name..." (Matthew 6:6-9, emphasis added).

If you are a parent, you can imagine how discouraging it would be if your children only talked to you when they wanted something. Quite the contrary, we talk to our children to discipline, instruct, nurture, train, comfort, encourage, guide, and teach. Our relationship with our heavenly Father is much the same. We are called children of God, and He longs to gather us under His wing like a mother hen and speak to us in the quietness of prayer. Our heavenly Father is always available and attentive, compassionate and caring, interested and involved.

Sometimes God wants to speak to us in our times of prayer simply to tell us how deeply He loves us. I will never forget a time of prayer I spent with a group of women just before I was to speak at an event. I had flown to Tennessee and moments before I went out to minister to the women who had gathered at the church, the leadership team held hands and prayed together. As one woman prayed, she said that God had shown her that very day that I was very precious to Him. God's love washed over me, and tears began to spill down my face. God loved me! He loved me! See, that's the message that I was going to share with those women at the conference, but in the hustle and bustle of preparation, God wanted to remind me that He loved me too.

Alarming News

I love sitting outside on my patio and spending time alone with God. However, not all of the sounds in my neighborhood are pleasant. There's the clatter of trash being dumped in the garbage truck, the crashing of glass being tossed into the recycling bins, the occasional whizzing by of a driver disregarding the 25 mph speed limit signs posted at the corner. A fairly new noise that has invaded the tranquility of neighborhoods all across America is that of alarm systems. When I hear the familiar blaring siren coming from first one house and then another in the wee hours of the morning, I usually think, "Oh, Fred forgot to deactivate his security system before letting the dog out again this morning." Never once has the siren caused me to jump to attention, thinking a home was being burglarized. Regardless of how ineffective the sirens might be, I admit that we have one too—and not just at our home, but at my husband's office as well.

Steve's office bears a striking resemblance to our home. It is a colonial brick two-story structure nestled in a stand of shade trees. There's the raised-paneled wooden front door, shutters beside the paned windows, and boxwoods surrounding the perimeter. Under the overhang of the far west gable is attached the blaring apparatus for the office security system.

The backyard of Steve's office was once a woodsy barrier that adjoined a street that some of our city's most prominent leaders called home. I am sure they were sickened to see bulldozers, backhoes, and concrete mixers intrude on the serenity they had cherished for some 30 years. I know I would have been. But progress moved in and an office park went up. The developers were kind enough to leave a thick stand of trees to keep the offices out of plain view of the homes a stone's throw away. But they still had to endure the noise. One such intrusion was the alarm systems.

Our alarm system was very sensitive at first. If a thunderclap shook the building the tiniest bit, the alarm would sound. If the wind whipped around the corner with unusual force, the jolted window would cause the blast to blow. Besides causing Steve great consternation because of police calls in the middle of the night, it robbed the neighbors of a good night's sleep.

One Saturday just before we were to move in, we were at the office cleaning up construction debris while the painter put the finishing touches on the interior trim. The doors were open to vent the paint fumes, so one of our new neighbors walked right on in. I could tell he was not happy. In his arms he held his blond two-year-old curly-headed grandson.

"Are you the owners of this building?" he demanded.

"Yes, we are. Can I help you?" Steve replied.

"I certainly hope so. I am tired of that alarm system going off in the middle of the night. I keep my grandson from time to time, and it scares him to death. We've been awakened several times, and I want this to stop."

The painter, standing on a ladder, held the paintbrush in his hand with a look of sheer terror on his face.

"I'm so sorry," Steve said. "We have had trouble with the security system. It goes off at the slightest vibration. The company is supposed to come by on Monday to adjust it. Until then, we'll just keep it turned off."

"Thanks. I'd appreciate that," the man said as he walked out of the building.

"What's wrong?" I asked the painter, who was still standing motionless like a stunned deer staring into a car's headlights.

"Ma'am, do you know who that was?" he asked.

"Yes, I do. He's a very prominent evangelist in this town. Why, have you heard him preach before?" I queried.

"Ah, no, ma'am. But if I were you, I wouldn't make that guy mad. He's got a direct line to God!"

I laughed and reassuringly said, "Oh, honey, don't worry about that. I've got a direct line too!"

The painter looked alarmed! How could I say such a thing? After all, he had not seen my picture in the paper lately, and I'm sure he didn't believe me.

"As a matter-of-fact, you can have one too," I continued.

I had to chuckle at this fellow's idea of God's hierarchy among the saints. But Romans 2:11 assures us that with God there is no favoritism. The Bible goes on to say, "There is neither Jew nor Greek, there is neither slave nor free man, there is neither male nor female; for you are all one in Christ Jesus. And if you belong to Christ, then you are Abraham's offspring, heirs according to the promise" (Galatians 3:28-29 NASB). I like to think of it this way: Whether you are a painter, an evangelist, a homemaker, a doctor, a roofer, a missionary, or a waitress, God loves us all the same and we have a direct line to Him available at all times. When we pray, God listens—no matter what our station in life.

"Call to Me," He says, "and I will answer you, and I will tell you great and mighty things, which you did not know" (Jeremiah 33:3 NASB).

The Purpose of Prayer

Prayer is not meant to change God's mind, but to change us and align our thinking with God's. When we begin our prayer with praise, we take the focus off ourselves and fix it on God. When we pray for God's will to be done, we take the focus off our desires and fix it to God's desires for our lives.

Jesus taught His disciples to pray, "Your will be done on earth as it is in heaven." For those who recite what we've come to know as the Lord's Prayer on a regular basis, it is very important that we never take those words for granted or treat them like a doxology to a commonplace prayer. The will of God is the cornerstone, the focus, and the ultimate purpose of prayer. Jesus Himself prayed for God's will to be done. In the Garden of Gethsemane, just before His arrest, Jesus prayed, "Father, if you are willing, take this cup from me" (Luke 22:42). His prayer was so intense, capillaries burst and droplets of blood trickled down His forehead. And yet, as much as He would have welcomed redemption in another way other than the cross, Jesus prayed, "yet, not my will, but yours be done."

I am so thankful that God has not answered each of my requests with a yes. My life would be much different than it is today—and I don't mean for the better. How thankful I am for my heavenly Parent who knows what's best for me! He has plans that are above and "beyond all that we ask or think" (Ephesians 3:20 NASB), and in order to hear God speak through prayer, we must allow ourselves to think beyond our limited knowledge, to see beyond our limited vision, and to believe beyond our limited understanding.

Prayer turns our focus toward God and allows Him to rearrange our priorities. It is more than unloading our burdens and enumerating our desires. Prayer sets our agenda. Did you ever notice that Jesus didn't set His agenda and then ask God to bless it? No, He did only what the Father told Him to do. He "had to go" to Samaria, the next town, and to Zacchaeus's home for dinner. He also had to delay His journey to see His ailing friend, Lazarus, until he had been dead for four days. Why? Because that's what His Daddy told Him to do.

When God Says Yes

The Bible is filled with promises regarding God answering our prayers.

> I tell you the truth, if you have the faith and do not doubt, not only can you do what was done to the fig tree, but also you can say to this mountain, "Go, throw yourself into the sea," and it will be done. If you believe, you will receive whatever you ask for in prayer (Matthew 21:21-22).

> "Have faith in God," Jesus answered. "I tell you the truth, if anyone says to this mountain, 'Go throw yourself into the sea,' and does not doubt in his heart but believes that what he says will happen, it will be done for him. Therefore I tell you, whatever you ask for in prayer, believe that you have received it, and it will be yours. And when you stand praying, if you hold anything against anyone, forgive him,

so that your Father in heaven may forgive you your sins"
(Mark 11:22-26). (Moving a mountain was symbolic of
moving a difficult situation.)

Ask and it will be given to you; seek and you will find;
knock and the door will be opened to you. For everyone
who asks receives; he who seeks finds; and to him who
knocks, the door will be opened. Which of you fathers, if
your son asks for a fish, will give him a snake instead? Or
if he asks for an egg, will give him a scorpion? If you then,
though you are evil, know how to give good gifts to your
children, how much more will your Father in heaven give
the Holy Spirit to those who ask him! (Luke 11:9-13).

If you remain in me and my words remain in you, ask
whatever you wish, and it will be given you (John 15:7).

Until now you have not asked for anything in my name.
Ask and you will receive, and your joy will be complete
(John 16:24).

Dear friends, if our hearts do not condemn us, we have
confidence before God and receive from him anything we
ask, because we obey his commands and do what pleases
him (1 John 3:21-22).

This is the confidence we have in approaching God: that if
we ask anything according to his will, he hears us. And if we
know that he hears us—whatever we ask—we know that
we have what we asked of him (1 John 5:14-15).

When you ask, you do not receive, because you ask with
wrong motives, that you may spend what you get on your
pleasures (James 4:3).

Everything was going along fine until I added that last verse in
there! Did you notice a few stipulations to our prayers? We must
pray according to God's will, ask with pure motives, be pure in
heart, forgive any who have offended us, obey His commands, ask

in faith, and pray in Jesus' name. Anything less, and we may not hear a response from God.

David wrote, "Delight yourself in the LORD and he will give you the desires of your heart. Commit your way to the LORD; trust in him, and he will do this: He will make your righteousness shine like the dawn, the justice of your cause like the noonday sun. Be still before the LORD and wait patiently for him" (Psalm 37:4-7). As we learn to trust in the Lord, our hearts begin to meld together and our desires become His desires. As we grow in Christ, we become more conformed to His image in our thoughts, words, and actions.

Sometimes it is easy to look at the heroes of the Bible and think that they are vastly different from you and me. However, time and time again, God confirms that they are not superhuman but simply human. James records, "Elijah was a man just like us. He prayed earnestly that it would not rain, and it did not rain on the land for three and a half years. Again he prayed, and the heavens gave rain, and the earth produced its crops" (James 5:17). Now, Elijah didn't pray for a drought on a whim of his desire. This was God's punishment on a rebellious nation and God put it in Elijah's heart to pray. But what excites me the most about this verse is that "Elijah was a man just like us." Just like us! "The prayer of a righteous man is powerful and effective" (James 5:16).

Again, in Acts 3, Peter and John met a lame man on their way to the temple. The man held out his hand and asked for money, but Peter gave him more than money, he gave him movement. "Silver or gold I do not have, but what I have I give you. In the name of Jesus Christ of Nazareth, walk" (Acts 3:6). The man went walking and leaping and praising God! As the people looked on in astonishment, Peter proceeded to preach one of his most powerful sermons. Here's my favorite part of the story: "When they [the religious rulers] saw the courage of Peter and John and realized that they were unschooled, ordinary men, they were astonished and they took note that these men had been with Jesus" (Acts 4:13). I don't know about you, but that verse makes me want to start walking and leaping and praising God! Oh, that people would say that about you and me. "When they saw the courage of (put your name here), and realized that she was an unschooled, ordinary woman, they were astonished and they took note that she had been with Jesus!"

(Excuse me while I leap for joy a moment or two. Okay, now I'm back.)

When God Says No

As with any good parent, God's answers to our requests are not always yes. When God says no, we must accept the fact that Father knows best. In my own life, my desire was to have three or four children. I conceived my first child with no problem. Little did I know at the time that Steven would be my only child. For years my husband and I prayed for more children. We traveled down the road of infertility doctors, diagnostic procedures, and timed intimacy, which is anything but intimate. As hard as it was for me to accept, God said no. Do I understand God's decision completely? No, I do not. But I've come to realize that He doesn't owe me an explanation. God is God. He does what He pleases, and I must trust Him. When we can't see His hand, we must trust His heart. I have come to the same conclusion as David, the psalmist, "One thing God has spoken, two things have I heard: that you, O God, are strong, and that you, O Lord, are loving" (Psalm 62:11-12). God is strong—He can do anything. God is loving—He will always do what is in our best interest.

Have you ever considered that God said no to His own Son, Jesus? Just before His arrest, Jesus prayed, "My Father, if it is possible, may this cup be taken from me" (Matthew 26:39). And yet, God did say no. Jesus went to the cross. God knew it was the only way. He loves you and me that much.

We can be assured that if God does say no to our requests, it is for the same reason—He loves you and me that much.

When God Says Wait

Sometimes God says yes, sometimes God says no, and sometimes God says wait. Abraham had to wait 25 years before God fulfilled His promise to give him a son. David had to wait many years before God fulfilled His promise to make him a king. Joseph had to wait many years before God fulfilled His promise to lift him up so he could rule over his brothers. The people of Israel had to wait several hundred years before God fulfilled His promise to send them a Savior. Waiting is difficult. As women, we tend to want to take matters in our own hands and make things happen, and we only have to look as far as the Garden of Eden to see what can happen when we do. Sarah grew weary of waiting for God to fulfill His promise to provide her a son and took matters in her own hands. She sent Abraham into her tent with her servant, Hagar, and they gave birth to trouble. Rachel grew weary of waiting on God to fulfill His promise to bless her second born over her first. She took matters into her own hands, dressed Jacob up as Esau, and deceived her nearly blind husband, Isaac. As a result, Jacob became a deceptional prodigy.

Waiting is one of the most difficult tasks of being a woman who listens to God. But of one thing we can be assured: God is never early and He is never late. Oh, it may feel as though He is. It appeared so to Mary and Martha, who were waiting for Jesus to come and heal their brother, Lazarus. When Mary and Martha sent word to Jesus that Lazarus was sick, He waited two days before He made the journey to Bethany to see them. When Jesus finally arrived, Lazarus had been dead for four days.

Mary, Martha, and the townspeople were mourning and wailing over their loss. "If only You had been here," Martha said. Yes, in her mind, Jesus was too late. But Jesus knew exactly what He was doing and when He was to do it. It was His Father's plan all along to raise Lazarus from the dead. After four days, the dead body would have begun to decay. How like God to wait until a situation looks completely hopeless to bring about a miracle for greatest impact. Had He healed Lazarus right away, some would have believed. But when God raised him from the dead, many believed. Friends, remember this. God is not waiting to answer a prayer as one playing with our emotions. When Jesus saw the grief of Mary and her friends, He broke out in tears and wept. Jesus was deeply moved in spirit and troubled. It was difficult for Him to see the pain death had brought, and yet He knew the joy that was yet to come. This would not be the last time someone would roll away a stone to reveal a miraculous resurrection!

"Did I not tell you that if you believed, you would see the glory of God!" (John 11:40).

Oswald Chambers said, "Prayer is not a preparation for work, it is the work. Prayer is not a preparation for the battle, it is the battle."[1] God always answers our prayers, but not always in the way we expect.

Lassie Come Home

When I was eight years old, my prized possession was a collie named, what else, Lassie. Lassie was my shadow. She ran alongside me as I pedaled around the neighborhood on my pink-glittered banana bike. She slept outside the door of my one-room playhouse when my best friend, Wanda, and I "camped out." She protected me from dangerous strangers, such as the paperboy, the mailman, and the trash collector.

When the veterinarian told us that Lassie had an incurable skin disease and needed to be put to sleep, I was devastated. And even though she was my dog, my dad was almost as heartbroken as I was. He could not bring himself to purposely end Lassie's life, so he drove her out to an old farmhouse about 15 miles from town.

"Could you please take care of my dog for me?" he asked the old farmer. "She's got a skin disease, but I can't bring myself to put her down."

"Sure," the fellow agreed. "Just leave her here. We'll look after her for you."

I never did get the particulars. Did he pay the man? Was he a nice man? Did he have children? All I knew was that Dad had done the best he could.

Months later, Dad went by to check in on the old girl. "I'm sorry, Mr. Edwards," the old farmer said. "Lassie ran away a few days after you left her here. We've never seen her since."

Dad never told me Lassie had run away. But each time he drove into Tarboro, the town near where he had left her, he panned the landscape, looking for a lost dog that answered to the name of Lassie. Miraculously, one day he spotted a collie wandering around the street. Dad jumped out of the car, pulled his pipe out of his mouth, and called out, "Lassie, here girl. Come here, girl." As he clapped his hands together, the dog bounded toward my dad, almost knocking him off his feet. A flurry of fur, wagging tail, and sloppy dog kisses smothered Dad as the two were reunited. What a surprise we had that evening when Lassie came cruising home in the gray Buick.

"Lassie! Lassie!" I cried.

I had never seen such a welcome sight. As a matter of fact, her skin disease was completely gone, and her coat was thicker and more beautiful than ever. All was well with the world.

Two weeks later, my older brother was out wrestling with Lassie in the yard. Dazed and ashen-faced, he stumbled through the door.

"Mom, we've got a big problem," he said. "You know Lassie, well...well...she's not a lassie at all. She's a laddie. This dog is a boy!"

"What!" my mother exclaimed.

We ran outside and checked. Sure enough, she was a he. This was not our dog! No wonder her (his) coat looked so thick and healthy.

"Mom," I said, "if this isn't Lassie, then who is it? We've stolen someone's pet!"

Needless to say, we put ads in the Tarboro and Rocky Mount papers, but no one ever claimed Laddie. He seemed perfectly content at our home, so there he stayed.

Have you ever wanted something so badly—hunted, searched, and maybe even prayed—and then when you found it, you realized that maybe it wasn't exactly what you wanted, but it was definitely what you needed? I wanted my dog back. Laddie wanted a family. And for one little girl and a stray pup, God answered my prayer. As usual, His answer had an unexpected twist, but it was perfect in every way.

Prayer Is a Two-Way Street

I had been in Raleigh, North Carolina, on a speaking engagement when we received the news that Hurricane Floyd was making its way up the coast. The ladies quickly said their goodbyes and I hopped in the car to make the three-hour trip home. Already the rain was pelting my windshield and the trees were swaying in the gusty wind. A hurricane so far inland was quite unusual. Once I made it out of town and to the highway, I joined several thousand travelers trying to outrun and escape the storm. Men, women, and children as far as 200 miles away were on the road evacuating the coastal areas.

During my adventure, God and I had plenty of time for conversation. He showed me that my journey home was much like many people's prayer lives. I was stuck in a long line of evacuation traffic. My side of the highway was clogged with panicky people trying to get as far away from the storm as possible. However, on the other side of the highway, the lanes heading east, there was only the occasional brave traveler determined to get to his or her destination. I imagine that's how God sees His children pray. There's a loooooooong line of people calling out for help—that would be the evacuation lane. And then there's the sparse few people listening to what God has to say—that would be those heading in the eastbound lane. While prayer is a two-way street, many of us spend far more time on the street directing our prayer to God for help and far too little time on the street receiving His direction. But I have learned that what God has to say to me is far more important than what I have to say to Him, and I need to be praying in both lanes—speaking and listening.

When You Pray, Pay Attention to What Happens Next

I love the story about a man caught in a terrible flood. As he watched the waters continue to rise, he climbed to his rooftop and began to pray. After a few minutes, someone in a boat came by. "Hello up there. Would you like to hop in my boat and let me take you to safety?"

"No," replied the man. "I have prayed and I am asking God to save me." With that, the boat passed him by.

"God, please save me," the man continued to pray.

Just then, a man in a helicopter arrived and hovered overhead. "Hello down there. Would you like for me to throw you a rope and pull you up to safety?"

"No," replied the man. "I am praying for God to save me." With that, the helicopter flew away to rescue others in need.

The man continued to pray, "Lord, please save me." Just then a family came drifting by on a raft.

"Hello over there. We have room for one more in our raft. Would you like for us to paddle over to you and take you to safety?"

"No," replied the man. "I'm praying for God to save me." With that, the raft drifted along with the current, taking the family to higher ground.

The water continued to rise and just before the man was totally submerged he cried, "God, I prayed for You to save me. Why didn't You answer my prayer?"

"I tried," answered the Lord. "I sent you a boat, a helicopter, and a raft!"

How many times have I prayed but then missed God's answer? I dare not speculate!

Lost and Found

My husband, son, and I went to Cancun, Mexico, during spring break in 1996. The vacation was a fun family time, but the trip home was grueling. The airport was full of hot, sweaty, smelly vacationers anxious to return home. We were originally scheduled to leave Mexico at 5:30 P.M., but because of various delays, were rescheduled to depart at 8:30 P.M. However, the darkness of the night did not cloak the rickety appearance of our aircraft. My son kept insisting, "Mom, when we walked by the plane to get on, I saw duct tape on the left rear wing!"

The airplane was old, hot, and filled to maximum capacity. It didn't matter that the flight crew spoke little English because the plane was so loud that we couldn't hear what they said anyway. We couldn't even hear the person in the seat beside us.

We knew we were in trouble when we put down our tray tables and two of the three were broken. When the flight attendant demonstrated the emergency procedures, you bet we all paid very close attention. As a matter of fact, I don't think I ever remember seeing such an attentive group of passengers.

After we were finally airborne, the flight attendant announced, "Because of our flight delays, it will be necessary for us to make a short stop at the Orlando airport to go through U.S. customs. We are sorry for any inconvenience this may cause."

So at 12:00 A.M., 90 hot, tired, disgruntled passengers disembarked the airplane, checked their carry-ons through customs, picked up their luggage at the baggage claim, checked that luggage through customs, and then returned to reboard.

This wasn't too complicated, especially since we were the only people in the whole Orlando airport at midnight! There was just one problem. When we went to pick up our luggage, one of our bags wasn't there. It was missing, most likely somewhere back in Mexico. This was the suitcase containing my husband and son's clothes, most of which were dirty. We were a little upset but more concerned with getting home in one piece than with the one piece of missing luggage. Finally, we arrived in our hometown at 2:15 A.M. and filled out the necessary claim. Again, we were not terribly concerned. After all it was only clothes, and dirty clothes at that. (Except for my son's one new T-shirt that we had to go through customs in Orlando to check and declare.)

The next day, my husband went to reach for his Bible to have his quiet time, but the Bible was nowhere to be found.

"Honey, have you seen my Bible? I can't seem to find it anywhere!" As soon as he finished his sentence, he remembered. He had placed his Bible in the lost suitcase with the dirty clothes. Suddenly the suitcase was no longer unimportant. This was the Bible that I had given him on our honeymoon 15 years before, the Bible that I had rebound on our tenth anniversary, the Bible with notes on every page taken over 15 years of study. We began to pray. We called and asked others to pray. We had to get that suitcase back!

"Oh, Lord," I prayed. "You know how much this Bible means to Steve. Please have the right person find this suitcase and return it to us safely."

Just as I finished my petition, God spoke to my heart. *Isn't it amazing how the realization of what was* inside *the suitcase changed its value? At first the lost luggage was of little consequence, but after you realized what was inside, tucked among the dirty clothes, suddenly it had great importance. So it is with My children. You may look at someone and see only "filthy rags," but I see a beautiful creation and a possible dwelling place for My Son, and that makes him valuable to Me. You may look at someone and non-chalantly see a lost soul, but I look at the lost as someone who needs an intercessor—someone who will plead their case before Me and pray for them to be found.*

Never again will I look at the dirty, downtrodden, or the lost the same way. God spoke to me during my prayer time to remind me that each person has great value as a possible dwelling place of something very special, *Someone* very special, Jesus Christ, God's own Son. Now when I see such a person, I try to imagine, as though I had x-ray eyes, a little black Bible hidden somewhere among the clutter, and suddenly I can see them as my heavenly Father sees them—welcomed, valuable, and precious in His sight.

P.S. The airport courier delivered our suitcase four days later, Bible intact.

FOUR

God Speaks Through Circumstances

I'VE ALWAYS LOVED THE BEACH. My ideal day begins by heading to the sand and popping up my blue-and-white striped umbrella just as the sun peeks over the watery horizon. I escape into a freshly opened novel while sipping on a continuous flow of sweetened iced tea. Walking, reading, resting, and oh—people watching.

Besides enjoying God's creation, I also enjoy watching His creatures. You can learn a lot about human nature by observing people at the beach. Teenage girls position themselves strategically to be noticed by muscle-bound young men strutting down the sandy runway. Dads pass footballs to admiring sons who beam with delight at having some one-on-one time with their hero. Moms in skirted swimsuits look at bikini-clad teens in disgust while secretly lamenting bygone days of flat tummies and slender thighs. Little tots squeal with excitement at the sudden freedom to play in the sand with no one telling them to stay out of the dirt. Tiny feet are in constant motion like little wind-up toys running from mom to the water, and back to mom again. Have you ever noticed that no child under the age of four walks at the beach? It's a gallop, or a skip, or a sprint. But never a walk.

I was reclining in my lounge chair one beautiful, summer day, not reading but people watching. I noticed an Asian family on my immediate right. The small-framed mother was kneeling by her adult son and wiping the sand off of his feet with a towel. Then she "humbly" slipped his shoes on his clean feet. The young man was casually reading a book, never looking up, as his subservient mother waited on him, literally, hand and foot.

"How disgusting," I thought to myself. "This is America. Let the boy wipe his own feet." I believe in being submissive, but this was taking it a little bit too far. I made a mental note to have a talk with this woman.

With that thought, I closed my eyes and took a little snooze while the sea breeze gave me a gentle massage.

That evening, after showering away all traces of salt and sand, my husband, son, and I headed for the elevator to search out a restaurant for dinner. Who should be sharing the ride down with us but the family with the feet-wiping mother? We reached the ground floor and the men parted to let the mother pass. Then her son awkwardly followed behind. His legs were fitted with metal braces and his arms were cuffed with metal crutches. With great effort, he swung his arms forward and propelled his lower body toward the door. Straining to keep up, his robot-like jerking movements maneuvered him down the hallway and out the door.

The elevator emptied. A loud silence screamed in my ears. I felt as convicted as I've ever felt in my life. Part of me still feels the shame, and I can hardly believe I'm sharing this with you today. I wanted to stay in that elevator and ride back up to my room and fall on my knees. Subservient indeed. Now a whole new list of words describing this mother flooded my mind: loving, tender, caring, pained, sacrificing, and brave.

"Lord," I prayed, "Forgive me for jumping to conclusions and making quick judgments. Forgive my critical spirit. Bless that mother and her child. Give him strength of body and her strength of heart. Thank You for speaking to me today through this mother and son. Create in me a clean heart, O God. How quick I can be to judge. Help me see the world through Your eyes."

You can learn a lot about human nature by watching people on the beach.

God speaks through His Word, through the Holy Spirit, through prayer, and He speaks through circumstances. Circumstances can take many forms: a seemingly disastrous day, a broken-down car, a bad report from a medical examination, an opportunity to minister, the death of a loved one, a celebration, an act of disobedience, a failure, a success, or a miraculous recovery. "The key is not the occurrence itself but the presence of the Holy Spirit as he communicates through life events. This does not mean we should seek a hidden meaning behind every traffic jam or thunderstorm. It does mean we should be sensitive to what God might be saying during the course of events in our day."[1] We cannot say that God speaks through every circumstance in our lives. But we can say that He speaks through some. Our responsibility is to pay attention, turn aside, and be attentive when He does speak so we can listen to what He is saying.

Frederick Buechner pointed out,

> Every once in a while life can be very eloquent. You go along from day to day not noticing very much, not seeing or hearing much, and then all of a sudden when you least expect it, very often, something speaks to you with such power that it catches you off guard, makes you listen whether you want to or not. Something speaks to you out of your own life with such directness that it is as if it calls you by name and forces you to look where you have not had the heart to look before, to hear something that maybe for years you have not had the wit or the courage to hear.[2]

That is precisely what happened in my own life as I watched the young man exit the elevator with braces on his arms and legs. I was forced to look at my own sin—my tendency to swiftly pass judgment on others.

I think I understand what the prophet Isaiah meant when he said, "The LORD spoke to me with his strong hand upon me" (Isaiah 8:11). Sometimes it's a gentle nudge, but sometimes it's a strong hand upside the head or across my backside.

Don't Miss It!

Romans 8:28 says, "We know that in all things God works for the good of those who love him, who have been called according to his purpose." That good could be knowing God more intimately, being conformed to the image of Christ more completely, understanding the Scriptures more clearly, communing with the Spirit more intimately, falling in love with Him more dearly. God often allows or orchestrates certain circumstances in our lives in order to draw us into dependency on Him and intimacy with Him.

All day long God is working in and around us. It is so easy to simply go about the task of living without seeing God's handprints on our circumstances and footprints on our paths. When we see life as a to-do list to check off, or random acts of fortune to celebrate, or misfortune to endure, we will miss seeing God and hearing His voice as the scarlet thread that connects the moments and the days of our lives. Frederick Buechner noted, "All the absurd little meetings, decisions, inner skirmishes that go to make up our days. It all adds up to very little, and yet it all adds up to very much. Our days are full of nonsense, and yet not, because it is precisely into the nonsense of our days that God speaks to us words of great significance."[3]

When Jesus came to earth in human form, He had a definite plan and purpose. First John 3:8 tells us, "The reason the Son of God appeared was to destroy the devil's work." Another version says, "The reason the Son of God was made manifest (visible) was to undo (destroy, loosen, and dissolve) the works of the devil [has done]" (AMP). Even though His plan and purpose were clearly stated, Jesus "turned aside" when His Father placed someone in His path. Jesus turned aside to care for the woman caught in adultery and spoke to the Pharisees about forgiveness. He turned aside to heal a blind man and spoke about the reason the man had been blind from birth. He turned aside to bless children, even though the disciples tried to shoo them away. He turned aside to question the person who had touched the hem of His garment and spoke words of encouragement and healing to a woman who had been bleeding for 12 years. He turned aside to speak to a curious Zacchaeus perched in a tree. He turned aside to woo a frightened and insecure 14-year-old girl and welcome her with open arms—me.

Jesus paid attention to the circumstances of those around Him as He went from one place of ministry to the next. He noticed a woman mourning in a funeral procession for her only son, a woman drawing water by a well, a lame man lying by a pool, and a blind man crying out by the side of the road. To those looking on, they may have seen each of these situations as an interruption in Jesus' busy schedule, but Jesus saw them as divine appointments.

Think of how God spoke through the disciples' circumstances to reveal Jesus' true identity. Jesus stood in the midst of a horrific storm, raised His hands and said, "Peace, be still" (Mark 4:39 KJV). The storm stopped as quickly as it had begun. What did the disciples learn about Christ? Five thousand hungry men along with women and children gathered on a hillside. Jesus took five loaves and two fish and commenced to serve them dinner. What did the disciples learn about Christ? A woman caught in adultery was brought to Jesus for condemnation. Instead of condemning her, Jesus forgave her. What did the disciples learn about Christ? In each incident, God used circumstances to teach about His character and His ways.

It is so easy to miss God speaking through our circumstances. Jesus' first miracle occurred at a wedding in Cana. As you may recall, Jesus, His mother, and His disciples were present when the host ran out of wine. Jesus' mother mentioned this to Jesus, fully expecting Him to do something about it. She turned to the servants and said, "Do whatever He tells you" (John 2:5).

Jesus then told the servants to fill six stone water jars with water to the brim. "Now draw some out and take it to the master of the banquet" (John 2:8). When the servants took the wine to the master, he called the bridegroom aside and said, "Everyone brings out the choice wine first and then the cheaper wine after the guests have had too much to drink; but you have saved the best till now" (verse 10).

Some noticed the miracle and some did not. Sometimes God speaks to us in very unlikely ways, and if we're not looking for it, we may miss it. Being in tune with His voice requires more than our ears to hear and more than our eyes to see. "He comes to us in ways that require the whole of us to respond, because it is to the whole of us that He makes His appeal."[4] Oh, how I never want to miss God working through my circumstances as I travel through life! *Lord, don't let me miss it.*

Recently, I was at a funeral for the father of a friend of mine. Amazingly, three of the deceased's nephews were preachers, and each wanted a turn at eulogizing Uncle Bob. There was a Baptist, a Pentecostal, and Methodist—a very interesting service. One of the preachers' stories about ol' Uncle Bob really tickled me. I've changed the names, but let's let nephew John tell the story...

"When I was a young boy of 17, I was working in the family business and didn't yet have my driver's license. Uncle Bob came over one day, took me by the arm, and said, 'Boy, it's time to go and get your driver's license.'

"But Uncle Bob," I argued, "I haven't practiced enough. I'm not good enough yet."

"Don't you worry about that, son," he said. "I'll teach you what you need to know on the way."

The two men, one young and nervous with clammy hands and the other older and determined with a knowing grin, drove over to the Department of Motor Vehicles. John parked the car, not between the lines, but right smack dab in the middle of two spaces with the line running under the middle of the car. He very nervously walked into the building, fumbled through the driving test, and miraculously came out with a certificate and a license.

"I always wondered how in the world I passed that test," the now older man mused. "But years later I found out. Uncle Bob knew the patrolman who administered the test."

Wow! I sat there on the edge of my seat! That was the gospel! Jesus takes us by the hand and tells us it's time to get started moving on with Him. "Follow Me," He calls. Sometimes we tell Him, "I'm not ready. I need more practice. I'm not good enough yet."

But Jesus says, "Don't you worry about that. Follow Me and I'll teach you what to do along the way."

If it were up to our own abilities, we would never pass the test to be a part of the kingdom of God, but the truth is, we do pass. Why? Because Jesus knows the One administering the test. He makes sure we pass.

Well, I was so excited about this parallel I was about to jump out of my seat. Had he been the Pentecostal nephew, I might very well have done just that. I kept waiting for pastor number three to tie in his story about Uncle Bob to the gospel—but he never did. He didn't see it. To him, it was just a cute story about one of his favorite uncles.

I was taken back to Henry Blackaby's quote that I mentioned earlier. "Right now God is working all around you and in your life. One of the greatest tragedies among God's people is that, while they have a deep longing to experience God, they are experiencing God day after day but do not know how to recognize Him."[5] *Oh Lord, make me a woman who listens to God! Don't let me miss it!*

Childhood Dreams

Little five-year-old Allan, dressed in worn denim bib overalls, tiptoed up to the corrugated metal building that had intrigued him for quite some time. For days the sounds of hammers and saws and the scent of freshly cut timber had tugged on his curious spirit. Today was Saturday, the workers were at home with their families, and the power saws lay dormant as if resting themselves. Allan pressed his nose against the dusty windowpane and saw mountains of lumber stacked from the floor to the ceiling. He crept around to the back of the building and slipped through the unsecured back door.

Allan knew full well that he would get in big trouble if his mama found out he had been poking around the millwork shop. But today he didn't even tell his three brothers or two sisters where he was going. Allan cautiously stole into the forbidden territory, past the warning and no trespassing signs, and pushed the heavy sliding door just enough to the right to squeeze his tiny body through.

Finally in the building, Allan stared in awe of the heavy machinery that engulfed him on every side. His small frame was dwarfed by the large worktables, storage bins, and shiny razor-edged circular saws. He walked over to a pile of sawdust that rested on the floor and ran his fingers through it as though it were freshly fallen snow. Underneath a large plane, curls of recently shorn wood shavings lay scattered in disarray. The smell of the raw wood permeated his senses in a way that he would not soon forget. On one side of the building lay roughly cut timbers. On the other, the sun's rays peered through the windows to spotlight smooth, raised-paneled cabinets of the finest quality.

His mischievous eyes followed the stacks of timbers as he wondered what it would be like to climb such a pile. As his eyes reached the rafters, he spotted something resting in the far corner near the ceiling. He walked over to get a better look and discovered a beautifully carved oak headboard and footboard. "Wow," he mused. "someone's gone and carved themselves a purty bed. I wonder who it's for?"

About that time, Allan thought he heard someone coming and scurried out the back of the building as fast as he could. However, the sights and smells of the millwork shop would always be with him.

Forty-five years later, Allan sat at his massive old wooden desk and gazed at his company's sign through the open window: People's Building Supply and Millwork Shop, Rocky Mount, North Carolina. His mind raced back to that little boy who ventured into that metal building in Spring Hope, North Carolina, so many years ago. Just yesterday, he had discussed purchasing the old rundown building to use for his overflowing millwork business. "I think I'll go back there and take a good look around," he said to himself.

When Allan walked into the musty building, he felt as though time had stood still. He could envision the piles of sawdust, the curls of wood shavings, and the bins of lumber. His eye followed the lines of the walls to the rafters above. He couldn't believe what he saw.

"I'll be dogged," he declared. Allan removed his pipe from his mouth, placed his jacket on an old rustic worktable, and began to climb up the steps that led up the bins to the rafters. There in the far corner, like a long-lost treasure, lay the oak carved bed that he had seen as a child.

Later that week Allan instructed some of his workers to rescue the bed from its hiding place. Knowing how much his daughter loved antiques, he brought it home—for me.

"Sharon," he said, eyes gleaming with delight. "I've got something I think you and Steve will like."

"Dad! That's great. Where did you find this?" I asked.

"Oh, it's a long story," he replied.

Dad gave me the bed just before Steve and I were married. We scrubbed, sanded, stained, and sealed the magnificent work of art until it had the luster of a much-loved antique. Today it stands proudly in my guest room and beckons many weary visitors. But to me it is much more than a beautifully carved bed. It is a symbol of how the course of a life can set sail from a young child's dreams, the rewards of determination and persistence, and the treasures that await each of us when we choose to look up.

Circumstances Can Be Misleading

While God speaks through our circumstances, it can be very dangerous to make decisions depending on what we see. We should never interpret Scripture through the lens of our circumstances; rather, we should interpret our circumstances through the lens of Scripture. For example, if you pray for someone and they are not healed, you cannot interpret that to mean that God does not heal. The Bible shows us time and time again that God does heal. The interpretation of that circumstance is that God is sovereign, and in that instance He chose not to heal.

Paul gives us a wonderful example of how circumstances can be misleading. Paul knew he was called to spread the gospel to the Gentiles. God spoke to Paul through a person, Ananias. "The Lord said to Ananias, 'Go! This man is my chosen instrument to carry my name before the Gentiles and their kings and before the people of Israel. I will show him how much he must suffer for my name'" (Acts 9:15). Paul knew he was called for a certain task; however, he met opposition at every turn.

He wrote: "I have worked much harder, been in prison more frequently, been flogged more severely, and been exposed to death again and again. Five times I received from the Jews the forty lashes minus one. Three times I was beaten with rods, once I was stoned, three times I was shipwrecked, I spent a night and a day in the open sea, I have been constantly on the move. I have been in danger from rivers, in danger from bandits, in danger from my own countrymen, in danger from Gentiles; in danger in the city, in danger in the country, in danger at sea; and in danger from false brothers. I have labored and toiled and have often gone without sleep; I have known hunger and thirst and have often gone without food; I have been cold and naked" (2 Corinthians 11:23-27). Now I don't know about you, but if all this had happened to me, I would begin to doubt whether or not I had heard God correctly. My tendency is to judge whether or not I heard God's voice according to the success or failure of my circumstances. But this isn't God's perspective.

We cannot always interpret seemingly negative circumstances as failure of hearing God's voice correctly. Jesus heard God's voice perfectly and yet went to the cross. Joseph heard God's voice clearly in a dream and yet was sold into slavery and thrown in prison. Sometimes the puzzle pieces of our lives may seem ragged and ill-shaped, but each piece fits perfectly into place when God is choreographing the design.

Charles Stanley wrote, "We must learn to live for the presence of God in every circumstance of life. A child of God, walking in the Spirit, is to look for the handiwork, the footprint, and the handprint of almighty God in every single situation of life. God is sovereign, and we are His children. There is no such thing as an accident in the life of a child of God. There are some things God may allow. There are some things that God sends. There are attention-getters that God brings into our lives, but there are no accidents."[6]

It is easy to see God in the exceptional things of life, but it requires spiritual maturity to see God in the mundane. Never think that life is anything less than God's appointed order. "All things were created by him and for him. He is before all things, and in him all things hold together" (Colossians 1:16-17).

In *The Problem of Pain,* C.S. Lewis said, "God whispers in our pleasures, speaks in our conscience, but shouts in our pain." *Whether gentle whisper or claps of thunder, speak, Lord, I'm listening.*

Guilty as Charged

It was the busy time of year for me. I had a hectic speaking schedule, going from Chicago to Colorado to California in a matter of 12 days with Parents' Weekend at my son's college tucked in between. The last of this whirlwind of events was the retreat in California, and God hadn't shown me yet exactly what He wanted me to share with these gals. I had only four days to study, pray, and listen to God's specific *rhema* words before traveling from the East Coast to the West Coast.

When I came home from visiting my son, I had a note from the government, an invitation of sorts, one of those that you can't refuse—jury duty! "Noooooooo," I cried as I read that I needed to report on the following Monday. "God, You love me too much to let this happen to me. You know I've only got four days before I have to go back out again."

I folded the letter and prayed for deliverance. My only hope was that when I called in the night before I was to report, the operator would say my number was not needed. That did not happen. When she read the list, my number was called.

"Okay, Lord, I'll report, but I know You love me too much to let me get selected to be on a jury."

When I arrived at the courthouse, I discovered that there were four cases being tried that day. About 120 of us good citizens waited in a room, most hoping our names would not be called. After three hours, I heard those two words I did not want to hear—"Sharon Jaynes."

"Okay, Lord, I'm one of 30 people called in this group, but I know You love me too much to let me be chosen to serve on a jury. Remember California in four days."

The jury selection was arduous. It was an armed robbery case and the defense and prosecuting attorney were taking matters very seriously. Twelve potential jurors were called, and my heart silently cheered! I was not one of them. But things started going quickly downhill. The two attorneys grilled the possible jurors. Had they ever been robbed? Had they ever used drugs? Did they know any district attorneys? Had they ever been arrested? Did they know the defendant? Twelve went up and five came down. More went up and more came down. Finally I heard the wonderful words, "Judge, we are satisfied with the jury." I was not one of them. No sooner had I picked up my belongings and started making my escape when the judge said, "Now we will pick the alternate."

"Okay, Lord, You love me too much..."

"Sharon Jaynes."

Downcast and defeated I approached the jury box. For the next few minutes I told both attorneys all the reasons why I would be a poor choice. "I know several DAs. I had a friend who went to prison for cocaine possession and I thought the judge was way too lenient on him. I've been robbed—twice!"

No matter. I was on. As an alternate, I had to show up every day, but I did not get to deliberate or cast a vote. I just had to sit there and watch!

As discouraged as I was to be spending my precious few days at the courthouse, I must say the trial was a bit entertaining. A man, the accused, got off work at 5:00 in the afternoon. Over the next 12 hours, he consumed two-fifths of Wild Irish Rose wine, one-fifth of liquor, snorted crack cocaine, smoked marijuana, and drank a case of beer. Sometime the following morning, he had the stamina to walk in and rob a convenience store.

The store employee said the would-be robber walked in with a gun under his jacket, pointed it his way, and said, "You know what this is. You know what I'm doing here. Don't do anything stupid." The store owner calmly took the money from the cash register and placed it on the counter, the man tucked the bills into his pant leg, ordered the attendant to face the opposite direction, and then made his way to his car for the escape. When the attendant turned and faced the window, he saw the license plate and noted it for the police.

The would-be robber took the stand and told his side of the story. He had been out partying all night, got hungry, went to the convenience store to buy a muffin, and discovered he didn't have enough money. He went out to the car to ask his friend if she had any. She did not. He came back into the store to tell the attendant that he was sorry; he didn't have enough money to buy the muffin. (I thought this was very thoughtful.) When he went back in the store, the attendant opened up the cash register, placed the money on the counter, and said, "Here, take this." So he made a bad decision and took it. (I bet you'd like to know the name of a store that has such wonderful service!)

By this time, I needed a chin strap to keep my mouth from hanging open in disbelief. Did he expect us to believe that? Besides, we had the surveillance tape that showed him with something pointing at the attendant that looked as though it could have been a gun. He said his hands were cold and he had them in his pocket. (I guess one finger was frozen.)

The trial went on and on. Officers, detectives, and more officers. When I finally quit internally pouting about the terrible timing of my civic duty, I began to pray.

"Okay, Lord, I know You do love me and for some reason You want me here. All I can do is watch. You know I need to prepare for the upcoming retreat, but I know that nothing happens by accident. What do You want me to learn?"

I heard Him say, "Finally you're catching on. I have a great lesson for you to learn this week. Pay close attention."

My attitude changed. What had felt like an interruption was transformed into a divine appointment. God thought I needed to go on a field trip to prepare for the retreat, per se. As the trial came to an end, the prosecuting attorney approached the jury for her closing arguments. She paced back and forth just like ol' Perry Mason and recapped the facts with a freeze-frame of the surveillance tape as her backdrop. Then she placed her hand under her jacket as if pointing a gun at each of us. Meeting each of our eyes, she concluded.

"You know what this is. You know what we're doing here. Now, don't do anything stupid."

Boy, she was good. Of course, he was guilty, guilty, guilty. Of course, being that I was an alternate, I didn't even get to cast a vote or deliberate. So what was the point of my presence?

God spoke. *This is why you've been here this week. This is what I want you to tell those ladies in California. John 10:10 says that Satan comes to steal, kill, and destroy. He wants more than a muffin. He wants more than money. He wants to steal your joy, steal your peace, steal your freedom, steal your future, and steal your spiritual inheritance. When he attacks, he only has one weapon—lies. He points his gnarly finger at you and shoots out lies. The robber in this case didn't even have a gun. He just had his finger under his jacket. Satan doesn't have a real weapon either. He just points and shoots blanks—lies with no merit. When you believe his lies, he robs you. He empties out your cash drawer—change and all. This is what you tell them. I have blessed them with every spiritual blessing in the heavenlies (Ephesians 1:3), and I have given them everything they need for life and godliness (2 Peter 1:3). But some of them have been robbed. Some have placed their spiritual inheritance on the counter and allowed Satan to take it. Some have believed his lies and fallen victim to his tactics. Go tell them how to defeat the would-be robber and take the treasure back.*

You know what his weapon is? You know what he's doing here? Don't do anything stupid.

It was quite a field trip. God spoke to me in my circumstances and gave me a life lesson I won't soon forget. In all my studies, I couldn't have come up with a better example. Will God speak through our circumstances? Yes! He will take us to the laboratory of life to teach us some of His greatest lessons.

FIVE

God Speaks Through People

SHE WAS A SLIGHT BLACK WOMAN with deeply etched furrows in her weathered face. Her wiry hair, striated with shades of gnarly gray, was pulled back into a tightly wound bun. Arthritic hands, worn smooth by years of love, labor, and life, flipped through pages of neatly placed books on the store shelf.

I was 22 years old when I encountered this prophetess perusing shelves at a Christian bookstore in my hometown. Most likely my dress was too short, my shirt was too tight, and my face was too tanned. I was proudly strolling the aisles with my fiancé, giddy with young love and bouncing with the energy of a college coed. I must have looked like a silly little girl. At least that would have been my summation as I reflect on the scene today.

Steve and I were flipping through books on marriage when this little woman shuffled up beside me and placed her dark wrinkled hand on my arm. She looked me square in the eye and spoke.

"Young lady," she said, "the Lord has just told me that one day you are going to preach the Word of God."

That's all she said, but she stood there with her hand on my arm for quite some time and looked at me as though God were telling her more secrets than she was able to reveal.

I didn't know what to say, but somehow I managed a polite response.

"Thank you, ma'am, for sharing that with me," I replied.

She patted my arm, turned, and disappeared out the door.

When she was out of earshot, I said, "Steve, did you hear what she said?"

"Yep," he replied. And we both snickered in unbelief.

I wanted to tell her, "No, ma'am. You see, this is my fiancé. We are about to be married in a few weeks. He's going to be a dentist and I am a dental hygienist. I'm going to help him start his practice, and in three years we are going to start a family. In five years we are going to build our dream house and then have three more children. I'm not going to 'preach the Word of God.' I think you must have heard God incorrectly. Perhaps He was directing you to the lady one aisle over." Like Sarah when God told her husband she was going to have a baby in her old age—I laughed.

That was almost a quarter of a century ago, and now her prophecy has come to fruition. Oh no, I'm not a preacher in a church, but I do share God's Word all over the world on the radio, through published books, and at women's conferences. I guess that is preaching in a sense.

Just the other day I was praising God for how He has allowed me to be used in ministry to share the hope of the gospel to a hurting world. "Are you surprised?" I heard Him say. "I sent one of My prophetesses to tell you 22 years ago." I had not thought about that woman in many years, but upon His prompting, the scene replayed frame by frame in my mind.

"That's right. You did!" I said, smiling.

I then realized that this little lady had been a woman who listened to God. I can imagine the argument I would have had with God had He directed me to deliver such a message to a young girl like me then. "Lord, are You sure? Her dress is a bit short. She looks as though she's no older than 15 and boy crazy to boot. And Lord, she giggles. Do You hear that? She giggles. Lord, are You absolutely certain this is the message You've given me for this mere child?"

Regardless of her misgivings, she obeyed. Regardless of my misgivings, when God called me to work with Proverbs 31 Ministries 15 years later, I obeyed as well. She was a woman who listened to God and one of my heroes of the faith.

A Word from the Wise

Another way we see that God spoke in the Bible, and still speaks today, is through other people. All through His Word we see examples of how God spoke to someone through another person. The most common occurrences were when God spoke through the prophets. Samuel, Elijah, Elisha, Ezra, Nehemiah, Isaiah, Jeremiah, Ezekiel, Daniel, Hosea, Joel, Amos, Obadiah, Jonah, Micah, Nahum, Habakkuk, Zephaniah, Haggai, Zechariah, and Malachi were all men to whom God gave a special message for His chosen people. God used Moses and Aaron as His mouthpiece for many years as He led the Israelites out of Egypt and toward the Promised Land. He used Jonah to warn the people of Nineveh of their destruction if they did not repent, and He used Nathan to confront King David about his sin of adultery with Bathsheba. In the New Testament, we see who God used the disciples, Paul, and various other Christians, such as Aquila and Priscilla, to speak His words and will to others.

While it is clear God spoke through the prophets, it is also important to note that He spoke through many others who were not seen as "official" prophets. For example, God spoke through Abigail, the wife of Nabal. One day while King David was traveling with his men, they grew hungry. He sent ten of his men to a wealthy, albeit foolish and wicked, landowner, Nabal, to ask him for some food and supplies. Nabal did not welcome David's men but responded, "Who is this David? Who is this son of Jesse? Many servants are breaking away from their masters these days. Why should I take my bread and water, and the meat I have slaughtered for my shearers, and give it to men coming from who knows where?" (1 Samuel 25:10-11).

This didn't sit too well with David, so he and 400 of his best men grabbed their swords and decided to pay Nabal a visit. One of Nabal's servants ran to Abigail and reported what her evil and foolish husband had done. "Disaster is hanging over us!" the servant rightly reported.

So God used Abigail. This wise and beautiful woman gathered bread, wine, veal, roasted grain, raisin cakes, and fig cakes. She loaded all the supplies on a few donkeys and met David on the road. Abigail approached David, bowed to the ground, asked for forgiveness on her foolish husband's behalf, and praised David for his valor and calling by God. (See 1 Samuel 25:14-31.)

Oh, it's such a great story of a wise woman. God spoke through her and averted the slaughter of all the males in her household, kept David from avenging himself and sinning against God, and secured her position once God took care of Mr. Foolish. Ten days after his near brush with death at David's hand, Nabal met death face-to-face at God's hand. And what of Abigail? She became the next Mrs. David.

Queen Esther was another woman through whom God spoke. After a period of prayer and fasting, the Queen went before King Xerxes to plead for the lives of the Hebrew nation. Through her wisdom, words, and willful obedience to her call, she was God's mouthpiece used to deliver thousands of men and women.

God uses many people to speak to us today: friends, pastors, teachers, strangers, and family members. In the book of Acts, two tent makers, Priscilla and Aquila, invited a well-known teacher, Apollos, over for dinner and explained to him the "way of God more adequately" (Acts 18:26). Am I saying that God used a woman to explain Scripture to a preacher! Nope. I'm not saying that. God did. Check it out for yourself!

When we are faced with a difficult decision, we are encouraged to seek out godly counsel. "For lack of guidance a nation falls, but many advisers make victory sure" (Proverbs 11:14). "Plans fail for lack of counsel, but with many advisers they succeed" (Proverbs 15:22). After Paul's dramatic encounter with Jesus Christ, God sent Ananias to speak to him. Paul was blinded by the light of Christ—literally. Jesus could have very easily healed Paul's eyes; however, He chose to speak through Ananias. "Brother Saul," Ananias said, "the Lord—Jesus, who appeared to you on the road as you were coming here—has sent me so that you may see again and be filled with the Holy Spirit" (Acts 9:17).

The book of Genesis tells us that God created man and woman in His own image. With that in mind, we should view every encounter with another human being as an opportunity to see some characteristic of God. It is hard not to be in a hurry when dealing with people. We tend to value commerce over community, accomplishment over accompaniment, and solving a problem over savoring a moment. Each day holds many gifts from God through the actions and words of other people. It is a great loss when we leave those gifts unopened or are too rushed to realize they are even there.

Have you ever lost a friend to death? I have lost a few. Katie was 50 when she died of pancreatic cancer. In the last four months of her life, as she watched the sun of her life set much too quickly, do you think she saw each day as a gift? Each contact with another person as a treasure? Oh, yes. So why should you and I be any different? Maybe this day will be our last. I'm not saying this to be morbid. I'm saying this to make us alert to life, to see each day as a present to be unwrapped and experienced and to meet each sunrise with expectant reverence and awe.

Drifting

It was supposed to be a sailing adventure for Loran and his youth group at Central Church. A friend of his procured three sailing vessels that resembled the *Niña,* the *Pinta,* and the *Santa Maria.* I'm not sure how much they resembled the ships that came across the Atlantic with Columbus, but they seemed just about as old.

When they left the dock, the sky was blue, the wind was brisk, and the teenagers were ready to sail the sea. However, by nightfall, a threatening gale blew in and the rolling waves grew to 15-foot walls of water, tossing the tiny boats like toys in a toddler's tub.

"Loran," the captain said, "this storm could mean big trouble for us. You're going to have to stay up all night and hold the wheel steady to keep the boat on course."

So all night Loran fought the storm. He kept alert. He prayed to the One who calms the seas and kept his eyes on the sailboats in front of him, one of which held two of his most prized possessions, his daughters. Hundreds of times, the boat shot straight into the air and then dashed into the inky water. But Loran held fast. It was a battle he was determined to win.

In the wee hours of the morning, the wind and rains came to a halt. The storm had passed and once again the boats cut a smooth path across the glassy sea. Everyone was exhausted from the rollicking waves of the night before, so the team decided to look for a lagoon in which they could drop anchor. One was found, and the three sailing vessels stopped for a few hours of rest and relaxation in the safety of the cove.

Loran jumped into the cool crystal blue water and suddenly realized how tired he was from the struggle of the night before. He turned over onto his back, closed his burning eyes, and began to float. Slowly the knots in his neck and back began to unwind and tension escaped from his aching muscles. The noises of the teens playing in the water were soon muffled and the only sound he heard was water splashing against his skin and the occasional call of a seagull. He was so relaxed he almost drifted off to sleep as his body drifted out to sea.

After some time, Loran looked up and noticed that he had drifted a great distance away from the rest of his party. They were playing happily in the water and had no idea he was gone.

"Okay, Lord. Help me get back," he prayed.

Loran swam and swam, fighting the water with all his might, but the receding tide was stronger that he was. After what seemed a lifetime, Loran was still a mile or so from his friends and family.

"Help!" he cried. But no one heard his distant cry.

"Oh, God! Don't let me die now."

Somehow, Loran finally made it back to the boat alive. As he lay panting on the deck, he realized a great truth. Over the past 24 hours, he had been in great danger two times—once battling the storm and the other drifting out to sea. But of the two, he was in more danger when he was carelessly drifting along than he was when he was alert and standing fast.

God spoke to me through Loran's story. Paul tells us in Hebrews 2:1, "For this reason we must pay much closer attention to what we have heard, lest we drift away from it" (NASB). Carelessly drifting can be a dangerous business, but storms keep us alert and ready at the helm. I need to be alert at all times and careful not to drift aimlessly along but listen as God speaks to me through the course of life.

God Speaks Through You

Yes, God speaks through other people, but have you considered that God will also speak through you? One of the main reasons God spoke in the Bible was so that the men or women would in turn speak that message to someone else. God promised David, "Open wide your mouth and I will fill it" (Psalm 81:10). He promised a very reluctant Moses, "Now go; I will help you speak and will teach you what to say" (Exodus 4:12). "You will receive power when the Holy Spirit comes upon you," Jesus told the disciples (Acts 1:8). "In the last days," God says, "I will pour out my Spirit on all people. Your sons and daughters will prophesy, your young men will see visions, your old men will dream dreams. Even on my servants, both men and women, I will pour out my Spirit in those days, and they will prophesy" (Acts 2:17-18). More and more I see God raising up women who are teaching His Word and speaking the truth of the gospel through various venues.

Perhaps you are thinking, *but would God speak through me?* Yes, dear one. If you are a woman who listens to God, He will use you to speak to others. He doesn't pick the superstars. God chooses ordinary men and women to change the world. He chose an ordinary shepherd (David) to be a king, an orphaned Jewess (Esther) to save a race from extinction, an exiled adopted prince (Moses) to lead the Israelites out of bondage, a young Moabite widow (Ruth) to further the bloodline of the Savior, a coward hiding in a winepress (Gideon) to lead the Israelite army, a Samaritan woman of ill repute (the woman at the well) to bring an entire village to Christ, uneducated fishermen (James and Peter) to spread the gospel, a seamstress and dealer of purple linens (Lydia) to begin the church at Philippi, and a tent maker (Priscilla) to explain the gospel to a preacher. These were very ordinary people who listened to and obeyed a very extraordinary God.

Believers in Christ are called His "ambassadors" (2 Corinthians 5:20). An ambassador is a person who represents someone else. We represent Christ to the world, and we do so by the words we speak. He may speak to you through other people—and He may use you to speak to someone else as well. I know of no better way to speak God's words to others than by giving them the gift of encouragement, prayer, and loving praise.

Henry Blackaby wrote, "When you believe that nothing significant can happen through you, you have said more about your belief in God than you have said about yourself."[1]

Oh, the power of a woman's words. We must be so careful with the words that we speak. As James said, our words, like a tiny spark, have the power to set an entire forest on fire and change the course of a life (James 3:5-6). I cry out with David, "May the words of my mouth and the meditation of my heart be pleasing in your sight, O LORD, my Rock and my Redeemer" (Psalm 19:14).

Calming the Storm

A storm was brewing somewhere off in the distance. I could smell the scent of summer rain mingling with the dry earth. Trees were beginning to wave their arms and fingers in warning as the breeze rustled through the leaves. Quickly, I closed my book and ran into the house.

"Bye, Steve," I called out as I ran through the kitchen, grabbing my pocketbook and car keys. "I've put off going to the grocery store all day, and now a storm's coming. I need a few items for Sunday lunch tomorrow, and I'm going to try to beat the rain." I said all of this in one breath as I dashed past my husband in a whirlwind.

"Bye," Steve called after me. "Be careful and slow down!"

Driving down the road, I was glad the grocery store was only a few miles away. Just ahead loomed dark clouds flashing heat lightning in the summer sky. Speedily, I whipped into the parking lot, dashed through the automatic doors, grabbed my three items, and zipped through the express lane. I was quick, but not quick enough. I had lost my race with the storm. Torrential rains poured from the sky in sideways sheets, blocking the parking lot from view. Other last-minute shoppers were waiting for the storm to pass, or at least ease up a bit. Conceding, I went back into the store to wait this one out. It was then I heard a baby crying—not an uncommon sound in a grocery store. But there was something about the cry that stirred my heart.

The cry drew my attention to a weary mother with groceries piled high in her shopping buggy, standing in the checkout line. Two carefree little girlfriends, about seven years old, stood on one side of her, singing, giggling, and clapping their playful hands together. I imagined they were having a sleepover, and my mind raced back to many such carefree Saturday nights years ago.

On the other side of the mother, in stark contrast to the playful duo, stood the crying little sister. Her sad eyes were bloodshot, her face was contorted with sadness, and her dress was moist from tears that dripped from her chin. It was then that I realized that while a storm was raging outside the building, there was a greater storm brewing within its walls.

There was something about the toddler's cry that pulled at my heartstrings. Was she tired? Was she hungry? I couldn't tell at first, but something or Someone told me to watch closely and I would soon find out.

The little girl, not yet two, held up her arms to her mommy, begging to be picked up, but instead, her mother jerked her from side to side.

"Didn't I tell you to shut up? Now be quiet," she barked.

With that, her crying grew louder. She then toddled around her mother and walked behind the checkout counter. Still wailing, she reached up her pleading arms to the cashier. The stranger, obviously uncomfortable, kept her eyes on the task at hand and acted as if the child were not there at all. She never made eye contact or acknowledged the urchin at her side.

The older sister, thinking the scene rather humorous, pulled her sibling out from behind the counter.

"Tasha, come out from there. You don't even know that lady," she scolded.

Still crying, little Tasha turned and noticed I was watching. We locked eyes, which to her seemed like an invitation. It was. Tasha walked over to me, wrapped her precious tiny arm around my knees and rested her wet cheek against my leg. As I patted her back, she put her thumb in her mouth and quieted her heart. I then understood the source of the cry. It was hunger after all. Hunger for love.

After a minute or two, Tasha pulled back, looked up at me, and held up her arms. Her mother, as well as everyone else held captive by the storm, was watching.

"May I hold her?" I asked the mom.

She nodded.

I picked up little Tasha. She nestled her head against my chest and continued to quietly suck her thumb as I swayed gently back and forth. Her hunger was satisfied, if only for a moment, as I fed her with my touch.

Tasha's sister and her friend came bouncing over, curious about this lady who held her sister.

"I like your dress," one said.

"And I like your shoes," said the other.

"I like your green velour shirt," I countered.

"I'd like to go home with you," the first one whispered.

I just smiled, but my heart wept. Perhaps there was a storm brewing in the sister's heart as well.

All too soon, the storm cloud passed and the pelting rain slowed to a drizzle. Reluctantly, I handed the toddler back to her mother, who most likely was hungry for love as well.

After bidding the giggling duo farewell, I dashed to my car. I waved goodbye as they watched me drive away—a smile on my face and tears trickling down my cheeks. The Holy Spirit had sent me, not only into a storm, but to calm a storm. It caught me off guard. I hadn't expected to encounter God in the grocery store. But I've learned that God speaks to us when we least expect it, in ways that require more than our ears to hear and our eyes to see. He appeals to our mind, will, and emotions because it is with our entire being He longs to commune.

Yes, Jesus still calms the storms—and sometimes He uses our arms to do it.

A Word to the Wise

It is important to realize that just because someone says they have a word from God for you does not mean they do. Many a Christian has been led astray by a well-meaning, self-proclaimed prophet or prophetess who shares what they think is a plan for someone's life. First of all, I do not believe that God would give anyone direction through another person solely. God will confirm His directives through His Word and by the Holy Spirit.

Sometimes God may use other people to bring our sin to our attention. That's what He surely did for King David when Nathan approached him in 2 Samuel 12. There is another incident in 2 Samuel regarding King David that shows great spiritual maturity, probably learned because of his encounter with Nathan. David was traveling to Bahurim, and a man from the same clan as Saul's family came running out to meet him. The man, Shimei, ran up to David, cursed him, and pelted him and his entourage with stones. When he couldn't find a stone, he simply picked up handfuls of dirt and slung it at the king. "Get out, get out, you man of blood, you scoundrel! The LORD has repaid you for all the blood you shed in the household of Saul, in whose place you have reigned. The LORD has handed the kingdom over to your son Absalom. You have come to ruin because you are a man of blood!" (2 Samuel 16:7-8).

David's men wanted to cut Shimei's head off, but David told them to leave him alone. He surmised that perhaps Shimei was cursing him because God had called him to, and they should let him be. All I can say is that David took these curses like a man.

The interesting thing to note here is that these curses were not from God! A few days later, the same man, Shimei, crossed over the Jordan, fell prostrate before the king and said to him, "May my lord not hold me guilty. Do not remember how your servant did wrong on the day my lord the king left Jerusalem. May the king put it out of his mind. For I your servant know that I have sinned, but today I have come here as the first of the whole house of Joseph to come down and meet my lord the king" (2 Samuel 19:19-20). David's men still wanted to kill the man, but again David said, "Leave him alone."

Wow. What a lesson. If someone has an accusatory statement about us, and claims it is from God, perhaps we just need to let God deal with that person. Do we heed the words? Yes, we do need to humble ourselves and ask God if He is calling us to repent and change our ways. I think we can pray, as David did, "Search me, O God, and know my heart; test me and know my anxious thoughts. See if there is any offensive way in me, and lead me in the way everlasting" (Psalm 139:23-24). God will reveal to us whether or not the words are from Him or from someone who is just letting off steam to make herself feel better. There is a litmus test for such accusations: Though God will not condemn us, He will call us to repentance. And secondly, His guiding principle for dealing with believers is always love.

What do you do when someone says, "God told me to tell you..." and that something includes or affects your life? It is hard to argue with someone who prefaces a statement with "God told me," and perhaps that is the hoped-for desire in some cases. Henry Blackaby calls this "spiritual bullying."[2] Just because someone says "God told me…" doesn't mean He has. We are told to "test the spirits to see whether they are from God" (1 John 4:1). Oh, how I love the Bereans. They tested or compared every word Paul preached against the Scriptures to see if they were true (Acts 17:11). Some use the words, "God told me to" or "I have a word from the Lord" as a justification for doing what they want to do. Hearer beware.

When we are trying to decide whether God is using someone to speak to us, it is important to examine the message and the messenger. Once again, God will never say anything that is contrary to His Word. For example, when Moses sent in the twelve spies to check out the Promised Land, ten came back with an evil report and said the land was filled with giants and unattainable. However, two of the spies, Caleb and Joshua, said that they most certainly could possess the land because God had already promised them success. Caleb and Joshua's report fell in line with God's Word. The report of the other ten men did not. Unfortunately the people listened to the ten with the bad report and never got to set foot in the Promised Land.

God's Word is infallible; men are not. My husband always reminds me as I study footnotes, "Remember, Sharon, footnotes are not inspired by God." He's right. God's Word is truth. We must be careful as we examine the words of others to determine if they are indeed from God.

As God calls us to accomplish various tasks, those closest to us may try to discourage us because of fear or lack of confidence in our abilities. Yes, we must seek wise counsel, but with the knowledge that we can do all things through Christ who gives us strength and that God doesn't always call the qualified—but He always qualifies the called.

Just a Bit of Burlap

It was just a bit of burlap peeking out from underneath the soil, but to Ginger, it was something that needed to be unearthed.

My golden retriever, Ginger, was about 11 months old when we left her home alone for the first time. My neighbor Cathy agreed to feed her and keep an eye on her while we were away. On the second day, I called Cathy to check up on her.

"Cathy, how's Ginger?" I asked.

"Well, Ginger's fine. But you know that new maple tree you planted in the back yard?"

"Yeah. What about it?" I asked.

"Well, Ginger dug it up. It's lying in the yard on its side."

I had heard of dogs digging holes in the yard—and I expected that. But digging up trees! This was new.

When we arrived home, we assessed the situation and discovered what she was really after. The new tree had its root ball covered in a burlap sack. When we planted it, a little corner of the canvas was left peeking through the ground. Ginger had pawed at it a few times, but never more than a scratch to the surface. While we were away, she crept over to the canvas and dug at it with all her puppy might. She probably worked at it for hours, flinging dirt in every direction. Finally, she accomplished her mission and the burlap was totally exposed! Of course, she gave no thought to the tree she had toppled in the meantime or the roots that were left to dry out in the hot sun.

Oh my, I thought as I stared at the poor little tree. *This is so similar to what people do to each other at times.* My mind wandered to friends I have known (and myself for that matter) who have been toppled for much the same reason. Perhaps someone has a little flaw that comes to the surface in plain view. Then someone else comes along and decides that the flaw is a nuisance and must be exposed at all costs. So they start digging and digging—flinging dirt in every direction, with no thought given to what all this digging is doing to the friend. The rough canvas may be unearthed, but unfortunately at the expense of the person who was exposed.

Lifeless, toppled, wounded—and for what purpose? To satisfy someone's curiosity and dogged determination to uncover a flaw.

Steve and I gently removed what was left of the burlap bag covering the root ball. We sat the tree back up and lovingly patted the soil back around its dried out roots. Then, because of its weakened state, we braced it with rope tied to stakes in the ground. I watered the tree daily, not knowing if it was going to recover from the trauma. In the end, the tree survived, grew, and even thrived.

Oh, that we would do the same for our toppled brothers and sisters in Christ: Stand them back up, reestablish their roots into the love of Christ, hold them up if necessary, and water them daily with prayer.

Thankfully, Ginger left the tree alone after that. After all—she never cared about the tree in the first place.

SIX

God Speaks Through Creation

THE SEA BREEZE BLEW THE TANGLES from my knotted nerves as a choir of various birds sang reveille to greet the day. Myrtle bushes, bursting with fuchsia blossoms, added splashes of color to the sandy landscape. Jumping fish performed acrobatic feats for an audience of one.

Perhaps my favorite place in all the world is the beach. God seems to speak to me through each intricately carved seashell, soaring gull, and majestic wave. On this particular spring morning, I had gotten up before the others stirred from their slumber to have a cup of coffee with the Lord. I sat rocking on the cottage porch surrounded by coastal beauty and watching the water of the lazy canal meander by. As I was talking to God and thanking Him for all the splendor of His creation, He urged me to look closely at a reflection in the water. My eyes followed the wavy reflection to the side of the canal where there stood two pieces of weathered wood, forming a simple cross. Upon closer inspection (as I turned aside), I realized that this was actually one end of an old forgotten clothesline, but to me it was much, much more.

I knew at that moment the beams were there just for me. The owner may have viewed them as merely part of a clothesline in disrepair, but this cross was God's reminder to me that in all the majesty of His creation, it is the cross of two wooden beams that remains the most majestic of all. Two simple beams display to the entire world for all time the surpassing greatness of His love, the incalculable riches of His grace, and the unfathomable depth of His mercy to all who will believe. More beautiful than any blooming flower, more melodious than any song of my feathered friends, more powerful than the surf of the sea—the cross.

When I stop and think about creation, I'm always amazed that God *spoke* the world into existence. He spoke and it appeared. His words were so powerful, they were the agent He used to create the universe and all it contains. *"And God said,* 'Let there be light'" (Genesis 1:3, emphasis added). *"And God said,* 'Let there be an expanse between the waters to separate water from water'" (Genesis 1:6, emphasis added). *"And God said,* 'Let the water under the sky be gathered to one place'" (Genesis 1:9, emphasis added). *"Then God said,* 'Let us make man in our image'" (Genesis 1:26, emphasis added).

Not only did God speak the world into existence, He used what He created to speak to man. David wrote, "The heavens declare the glory of God; and the skies proclaim the work of his hands. Day after day they pour forth speech; night after night they display knowledge" (Psalm 19:1-2). "When I consider your heavens, the work of your fingers, the moon and the stars, which you have set in place, what is man that you are mindful of him, the son of man that you care for him?" (Psalm 8:3-4).

In the book of Job, we find a man who lost everything dear to him except his life and his wife. Thoughout the book, Job questions God, his friends question his righteousness, and his wife encourages him to curse God and die. In the end, God finally speaks to Job, and Job hears him loud and clear. "Then the LORD answered Job out of the storm. He said: "Who is this that darkens my counsel with words without knowledge? Brace yourself like a man; I will question you, and you shall answer me" (Job 38:1-3).

"Where were you when I laid the earth's foundation? Tell me, if you understand. Who marked off its dimensions? Surely you know! Who stretched a measuring line across it? On what were its footings set, or who laid its cornerstone—while the morning stars sang together and all the angels shouted for joy? Who shut up the sea behind doors when it burst forth from the womb, when I made the clouds its garment and wrapped it in thick darkness, when I fixed limits for it and set its doors and bars in place, when I said, 'This far you may come and no farther; here is where your proud waves halt'? Have you ever given orders to the morning, or shown the dawn its place, that it might take the earth by the edges and shake the wicked out of it? The earth takes shape like clay under a seal; its features stand out like those of a garment" (Job 38:4-14).

For the next four chapters, God reminds Job of His power and might by recounting His miracle of creation. Oh, I wish I could write out each and every word God spoke to Job. Please go back and read chapters 38–41. Read them aloud. I believe our friend Job got an earful that day. God is great, my friend, and His creation shouts His greatest praise, if we will but turn aside and listen.

The New Testament also tells us that God speaks through creation. "For since the creation of the world God's invisible qualities—his eternal power and divine nature—have been clearly seen, being understood from what has been made, so that men are without excuse" (Romans 1:20). Everywhere we look we can see God's handiwork and hear His voice through what has been made. Just as the prophet Nehemiah prayed, "Let your ear be attentive and your *eyes open to hear* the prayer your servant is praying before you day and night" (Nehemiah 1:6, emphasis added), we can hear God speak through what our eyes behold!

A.W. Tozer once said, "He is by nature continuously articulate. He fills the world with His speaking voice." I believe God's voice is heard nowhere more clearly than through His creation.

Resting in the Palm

A few years ago, I fell in love with a beach cottage named "Barb's Folly." I adored the designer beach decor of periwinkle blue and yellow stripes and florals, the screened-in porch that hugged the back of the house, the inviting dark green rocking chairs, and the weather-worn dock jutting out over the lazy canal. As if imported from England, a six-foot square of grass was nestled in one corner of the yard framed by a white picket fence. The secret garden was complete with fuchsia myrtle bushes in full bloom, a beckoning weathered bench, and a cozy bird house with a half dozen portals. Seemingly out of place, the owners had transplanted a palm tree just inches from the second story screened-in porch and encircled it with the wooden steps that led to the dock.

On our first night at "Barb's Folly" we rocked on the porch and watched fireflies dance on the moonlit canal. As if to light a lone actor on a stage, a moonbeam fell across the palm tree and revealed a gentle stirring in its plume. When I moved closer, I discovered that a turtledove had built her nest at the top of the thatched tree trunk where the palm branches sprouted upward. Because we were on the second story, we were at eye level with Mrs. Turtledove. As I moved closer to her, she didn't budge but sat steadfast in her perch.

Early the next morning, before the rest of the houseguests stirred, I went on the porch to spend some time with the Lord. Mrs. Turtledove was there to greet me. I watched her. She watched me. Our eyes locked. We both blinked. A few moments later, Mr. Turtledove flew in and perched on the nearby railing. The couple exchanged coos, and then he flew over to his beloved. When she stood up to welcome him, I noticed two tiny eggs peeking out from under the stubble. It seems this was Mother's morning out and Daddy Bird was here to watch over the soon-to-be little ones. Mama Bird flew away and Daddy took over the incubation and protection of their eggs. After a brief time, Mama Bird returned and Daddy Bird went off to work for the rest of the day.

During our entire vacation, Mama Bird did one thing and one thing only: She rested in the palm, warming and protecting her two tiny charges. On the afternoon when a violent storm blew through with loud claps of thunder, crackling flashes of lightning, and pelting sheets of rain, she sat undaunted by the storm and unmoved as the trees bent in the wind. When the children ran up and down the stairs inches from her nest and leaned over the railing to get a better look, she appeared unalarmed by the stir of activity. While other birds, such as cranes, pelicans, and seagulls, performed great feats, swooped gracefully into the water, and strutted about parading their showy display, her feathers were not ruffled, and she continued undeterred in her calling.

On the last morning of our vacation, I was enjoying a final cup of coffee on the back porch and once again relishing in quiet time with God and His creation. Of course, Mrs. Turtledove was there to join me.

"God," I asked, "I know You put this bird here for a reason. What do You want me to learn from watching her this week? I don't want to miss it."

Then God spoke to my heart. It was contentment. I was watching a picture of contentment in fulfilling God's call. She was doing what God had made her to do for this season of her life, and she was intent and content in doing it. Regardless of the storms, regardless of what seemingly showy birds were doing, regardless of the endless stream of activity passing by her nest, regardless of the stares of others, she was unmoved from her task at hand.

"Is that it, Lord? Is that what You want me to see?"

Just as I prayed those words, Mr. Turtledove flew in for his daily visit. When his lady stood up to greet him, I noticed a piece of eggshell attached to her leg. She flew away with much excitement, and then I noticed a change in her nest. There lay two tiny downy hatchlings. The eggs had hatched, and it was as if God were saying to me, "Yes, Sharon. That's it. This has been My gift to you this week. Through My creation, you have seen a contented mother and the results of her commitment. You do what I've called you to do. Rest in the palm—of My hand. Don't get distracted by the world around you: the storms of life, the endless stream of activity, other seemingly more glamorous 'birds.' Be relentless in your call. In due time, I will cause your 'eggs to hatch' and all too soon they will leave the nest."

About that time my 6´1˝ teenage son sleepily stumbled out onto the porch. I'm not sure if he saw the tears in my eyes as I looked at his ruffled hair, sleepy eyes, and face that needed a shave.

"Hey, buddy," I said. "Look, the eggs hatched today."

Jesus Spoke Through God's Creation

Like Father, like Son. Just as God spoke through His creation, Jesus taught His followers spiritual principles by giving them living examples from nature. We don't know much about Jesus' boyhood. Luke simply states, "And Jesus grew in wisdom and stature, and in favor with God and men" (Luke 2:52). The word for wisdom used in Luke 2 is the Greek word *sophia* and means "skill in the affairs of life, practical wisdom, wise management as shown in forming the best plans and selecting the best means, including the idea of sound judgment and good sense. *Sophia* is in respect to divine things, wisdom, knowledge, insight, deep understanding, represented everywhere as a divine gift, and including the idea of practical application."[1]

Just as a daddy teaches a boy a skill such as how to change a tire, hammer a nail, or knot a necktie, I think God taught His Son the Scriptures through life lessons, daily activities, and nature. Jesus grew skilled in the affairs of life, and like His heavenly Father, He taught spiritual principles through practical examples to His followers.

Jesus instructed His disciples, "Consider how the lilies grow. They do not labor or spin. Yet I tell you, not even Solomon in all his splendor was dressed like one of these. If that is how God clothes the grass of the field, which is here today, and tomorrow is thrown into the fire, how much more will he clothe you" (Luke

12:27-28). He pointed to flowers, trees, vines, and weeds and said, "Consider this...look at that..."

When Jesus was explaining His death and resurrection to His disciples, He used the example of a seed. "I tell you the truth, unless a kernel of wheat falls to the ground and dies, it remains only a single seed. But if it dies, it produces many seeds" (John 12:24). In one of Jesus' most compelling sessions with His 12 best friends, He compared their relationship with Him to that of a vine and its branches. "I am the true vine and my Father is the gardener...Remain in me, and I will remain in you. No branch can bear fruit by itself; it must remain in the vine. Neither can you bear fruit unless you remain in me. I am the vine; you are the branches. If a man remains in me and I in him, he will bear much fruit" (John 15:1-5). These were examples that the men understood.

Charles Spurgeon, a famous English preacher from the 1800s, once said, "God seems to talk to me in every primrose and daisy and smile at me from every star, and whisper to me in every breath of morning air, and call aloud to me in every storm."[2]

Masterpiece by the Bay

I grew up on the East Coast and was excited when my family decided to visit San Francisco for our vacation. My heart's desire and prayer for each day was that we would see God's handiwork, hear His voice, and be reminded of His greatness as we ventured out like three eager explorers to discover new aspects of His creation.

After we arrived in California, we traveled south along the shoreline and were amazed at the 200-foot regal cliffs that rose from the earth, pushing heavenward with waves splashing at their feet. Then we traveled north and drank in the beauty of acres and acres of vineyards on grassy rolling hills in the Napa Valley wine country. We hiked through the majestic Redwood Forest and stood under 1000-year-old, 260-foot giants, dwarfed by their towering branches.

But the most amazing sight was in a place called Alcatraz. There in the middle of the San Francisco Bay, just a mile and a quarter from the sights and sounds of the beautiful city, sits a rock island, known by some as the "Devil's Island of America." From 1934 to 1963, Alcatraz was a prison where the country's most corrupt, incorrigible criminals were housed. Al Capone and Machine Gun Kelly were just two of the more colorful residents.

There is no road to the prison, so we took a ferry across the bay. As we taxied up to The Rock and stared at the shell of concrete walls, barbed wire, and iron bars, an eerie feeling crept over my body. Each of us picked up headphones and a cassette recorder and toured the prison while listening to the taped voices of various prisoners recount their days behind bars. I walked in a cell called "the hole," closed my eyes, and tried to imagine what it would be like in solitary confinement with no light, no sound, and no other voice but my own. My heart was heavy as I thought about the souls that passed through those halls, souls full of darkness, depression, and despair.

But as I rounded the final corner of the tour, I saw an amazing sight: a white-haired, 80-year-old grandfather, with crystal blue laughing eyes and a radiant smile that spread across his wrinkled face. A line formed as tourists stood waiting for him to sign his name and number on his autobiography, *Alcatraz from Inside*. This precious man before me was Jim Quillen, ex-prisoner #AZ586. He had spent ten years of his life, from 1942 to 1952, behind bars in this prison built to house the most dangerous criminals of his day. I looked in his eyes as we spoke. This was not the face of a dangerous man. What had happened to change his life?

I didn't have to flip many pages in his book to find the answer. In it he wrote, "It was only through the grace of our Lord Jesus Christ and His intercession that my life of hopeless incarceration was averted. His help and forgiveness permitted me to obtain freedom, family, and a useful and productive place in society." I went back over to Mr. Quillen and sat by his side for a minute or so. We chatted for a moment, and he autographed my copy of his book. Then God spoke to my heart, "You prayed that you would see My handiwork and be reminded of My greatness. This man is some of my best work."

On my trip to San Francisco, I was reminded of God's unchanging strength in the majestic cliffs of the shoreline and of His nurturing care as the Vinedresser in the hills of the wine country. I saw a picture of God's protective canopy over His children in the towering redwoods. But when I looked into Jim Quillen's eyes, I saw God's most incredible masterpiece: a changed life. "You shall know the truth and the truth shall make you free" (John 8:32 NASB).

Putting the Pieces Together

God speaks to us in many ways. In this section I have listed what I feel are the key ways He communicates with us on a daily basis. However, it is very rare that any one of these means will stand alone. They fit together like intricate puzzle pieces to form a beautiful picture of the intimate relationship God desires with His children. If we simply focus on one piece of the puzzle, we will not be able to take in the full scope of the landscape and may perhaps see life as though looking through a peephole in a closed door. God speaks through His Word, the Holy Spirit, prayer, circumstances, other people, and nature.

In *The Pursuit of God,* A.W. Tozer described how the puzzle pieces work in tandem:

> It is important that we get still to wait on God. And it is best that we get alone, preferably with our Bible outspread before us. Then if we will we may draw near to God and begin to hear Him speak to us in our hearts. I think for the average person the progression will be something like this: First a sound as of a Presence walking the garden. Then a voice, more intelligible, but still far from clear. Then the happy moment when the Spirit begins to illuminate the Scriptures, and that which had been only a sound, or at best a voice, now becomes an intelligible work,

warm and intimate and clear as the word of a dear
friend.[3]

I have not heard God speak through a burning bush or a bright
light from the sky or though an angelic visitation. He hasn't
spoken to me out loud, but He puts thoughts into my mind that
are so distinctly from Him that He might as well have. "Sometimes
a thought pops into my mind," said author Carole Mayhall, "a
thought so different from what I was thinking, or so creative I
never would have thought of it, or opposite to what I wanted God
to say to me. When that happens—and it lines up with God's
Word—I know I've heard His voice in a distinctive way..."[4]

Each of the stories are highlighted in the book as a testimony
of Carole's words. I couldn't have fabricated the lessons; I dare say
I would have missed them altogether. The stories and their lessons
come from listening to God's voice in the everyday moments of
life. "My sheep listen to my voice; I know them, and they follow
me" (John 10:27).

One night as the famous Bible teacher, F.B. Meyer stood on the
deck of a ship approaching land, he wondered how the crew
knew how to safely steer to the dock. It was a stormy night, and
visibility was low. Meyer, standing on the bridge and peering
through the window, asked, "Captain, how do you know when to
turn this ship into that narrow harbor?"

"That's an art," replied the captain. "Do you see those three
lights on the shore? When they're all in a straight line, I go right
in!"[5]

What a beautiful illustration of how we can determine God's
voice. He speaks to us in many ways, and when they all line up,
we can sail safely into the harbor and drop anchor.

PART II

Counterfeits and Imposters

WHOSE VOICE IS IT?

Do you remember playing the childhood game Pin the Tail on the Donkey? One child is blindfolded, spun around in circles, and then pointed in the direction of a donkey posted on the wall. As she makes her way to pin the donkey's tail in the correct position, onlookers yell which way she should go.

"Move to the right!"

"Move to the left!"

"You're getting cold!"

"Now you're getting warmer!"

"Go up a little!"

Some of the voices intentionally try to mislead the blindfolded person, but usually the player will try to pick out the voice of her loyal friend, someone she can trust, and block out the others who desire to distract her. As she inches her way toward the donkey and returns to him his tail, she removes the blindfold to see if she trusted the right voice.

As we become women who listen to God, we also must learn how to discern God's voice from the many others that are calling out to mislead and distract us. There are many voices, and we must learn who is friend and who is foe.

In the Bible, we learn that Jesus Christ has already won the victory over sin and death, and because we are God's children, that victory is also shared with us. However, until Jesus returns, we will continue to fight a spiritual battle on three fronts: the world, the flesh, and the devil (Ephesians 2:2-3). All three voices shout commands, and as soldiers of Christ, we must be able to recognize the voice of our commander and the voices of the enemy forces. Let's take a look at these three "counterfeits" to God's voice and learn how to recognize them.

SEVEN

The World's Voice

IN THE NEW TESTAMENT, there are three words for "world." One refers to the "world" as the collective group of people that God loves. We see this in John 3:16: "For God so loved the world that he gave his one and only Son, that whoever believes in him shall not perish but have eternal life." The other two refer to the "world" as our enemy. We see this in John 15:19: "If you belonged to the world, it would love you as its own. As it is, you do not belong to the world, but I have chosen you out of the world." This same reference to the "world" as an enemy is found in 1 John 2:15-16: "Do not love the world or anything in the world. If anyone loves the world, the love of the Father is not in him. For everything in the world—the cravings of sinful man, the lust of the eyes and the boasting of what he has and does—comes not from the Father but from the world." In both of these incidences, the "world" refers to "the organized system of temporal values that are opposed to the life of Christ in the believer."[1] It is human systems that oppose God's purposes—man's wisdom apart from Christ's.

From the time we are born, we are programmed by the world around us. From movies to media, education to entertainment, and even sometimes by friends and family, we are pushed to fit into cultural norms and expectations. As long as we are in the world, we will have the tension of discerning whether the wooings we hear are from God or from the world. Again, the only way to discern between the two is to know the truth found in God's Word.

It's not simply knowing the Word of God, albeit that is the first step. We must believe it as well. That may seem like a strange statement; however, there are many biblical scholars who know the contents of the Bible back and forth, up and down, but don't truly believe in God's power through those words. "This is the victory that has overcome the world," John wrote, "even our faith" (1 John 5:4).

When Paul wrote to the various churches in the New Testament, he wanted to make sure they knew his wisdom and his words were from God and not the world. "My message and my preaching were not with wise and persuasive words, but with a demonstration of the Spirit's power, so that your faith might not rest on men's wisdom, but on God's power" (1 Corinthians 2:4-5). Library shelves bulge with books on philosophy and self-help diatribes. Magazine racks are weighed down with the latest New Age wisdom, which changes as quickly as each new issue is printed, and television talk shows clutter the airwaves with weak attempts at mental and spiritual health. We are the sick trying to heal the sick, the blind leading the blind, and the lame trying to teach the mental cripple to walk. What we don't need is more new ideas. What we do need is a new life. We need God.

Paul goes on to say,

> We do, however, speak a message of wisdom among
> the mature, but not the wisdom of this age or of the
> rulers of this age, who are coming to nothing. No, we
> speak of God's secret wisdom, a wisdom that has
> been hidden and that God destined for our glory

before time began...We have not received the spirit of
the world but the Spirit who is from God, that we may
understand what God has freely given us. This is what
we speak, not in words taught us by human wisdom
but in words taught by the Spirit, expressing spiritual
truths in spiritual words (1 Corinthians 2:6-13).

Yes, we have to live in the world, but we are not to be conformed to the world. That's very difficult at times. I think that was
one of the main themes of Jesus' prayer for His disciples before He
went to the cross. All through John chapters 14–17, Jesus prays for
us to be in the world but not tainted or persuaded by world systems and ideas.

- The world says take inventory of your strengths.
- God's voice says when you are weak, then I am strong.
  (2 Corinthians 12:10)

- The world says get all you can.
- God's voice says give to everyone who asks. (Matthew
  5:42)

- The world says claim your rights.
- God's voice says give up your rights. (Philippians 2:5-11)

- The world says avoid pain at all cost.
- God's voice says take up your cross and follow Me.
  (Matthew 16:24)

- The world says only the strong survive.
- God's voice says only those who depend on Me will
  thrive. (Proverbs 3:5-6)

- The world makes decisions based on common sense.
- God's voice tells us to make decisions based on His
  Word. (Psalm 119:105)

- ❧ The world says this is as good as it gets.
- ❧ God's voice gives us the promise of heaven. (John 3:16)

- ❧ The world says seek happiness in your circumstances.
- ❧ God's voice says seek joy despite your circumstances. (James 1:2-4)

- ❧ The world says divorce if marriage gets difficult.
- ❧ God says what He has joined, no man should separate. (Mark 10:9)

Some of the most worldly people during the time of Christ were the Romans. Paul wrote to the church in Rome, "Do not conform any longer to the pattern of this world, but be transformed by the renewing of your mind. Then you will be able to test and approve what God's will is—his good, pleasing and perfect will" (Romans 12:2). The only way to distinguish between the world's voice and God's voice is...you guessed it...by developing a personal, ongoing, intimate relationship with Jesus Christ and knowing the truth found in God's Word.

God's Speedometer

I met my husband at a Bible study in college and quickly learned that he was a very frugal, industrious, and resourceful young man. On our first date, he came to pick me up in his ten-year-old Volkswagen Beetle, which he had purchased for $725. He says it was yellow. I say it was beige. Regardless of the color, this fine piece of machinery had several "remarkable" features.

I don't know if it was the weather or our excitement on our first date, but as soon as we got into the car, the windows fogged up. As we drove down Franklin Street in Chapel Hill, Steve asked, "Sharon, will you please get the defroster from the glove compartment and help me out so I can see?" I reached in the compartment to pull out the defroster: a small towel. Of course I was impressed with his great wit and was delighted to ride around campus, wiping the front windshield as we went along. (Isn't it amazing the perspective we have of inconveniences when love is new?)

Another amazing feature of Steve's car was its ability to plow through snow. In the South, it's a big deal when we get more than a few flakes because we're not prepared for big snows. So over our first spring break, when it snowed 18 inches, everyone was either homebound or on the streets sliding around the road and into each other. Everyone, that is, except Steve and his Little Engine That Could. We were the envy of all the shiny new cars on campus.

But perhaps the most remarkable feature of the VW was the speedometer. It didn't work. The speedometer broke when the odometer hit 200,000 miles and never left 0 again.

"Steve," I asked, "if your speedometer doesn't work, how do you know how fast you are going?"

"Well," he answered, "I never know for sure. I just have to pay attention to how fast cars around me are traveling and pace myself according to their speed. Besides, I can tell when to change gears and about how fast I'm going by how much the car shakes!"

So Steve traveled around town and on highways with no earthly idea of his exact speed. He was totally dependent on those around him in order to pace himself.

We were married ten months after our first date on a hot August day between the last session of summer school and fall semester. It was about 98 degrees the day Steve drove from Charlotte to Rocky Mount, North Carolina for our wedding weekend. (Did I mention that the VW had no air-conditioning?) He left Charlotte in the wee hours on a Friday morning to avoid the midday heat. Because it was so early, there was virtually no traffic. Now that may seem like a dream come true for most people, but remember, Steve needed traffic to judge his own speed. His points of reference were missing, and he began to sweat. On top of that, he was excited about getting to his bride and his judgment was a little impaired. (I just had to put that in.)

About two hours into the trip, Steve saw a blue light flashing in his rearview mirror, and his heart sank as he realized he was being pulled over by a state patrolman.

"Where are you going in such a hurry, young man?" the officer asked.

"Actually, sir, I'm on my way to get married," Steve replied.

The patrolman smiled as he handed Steve the ticket and said, "Well, don't let this ruin your day."

Your day! Steve thought. *What about ruin your insurance and your budget—the budget of a guy working his way through school who had to have a yard sale to go on a honeymoon!*

When Steve told me his story, I was really angry at that patrolman. But the truth is, cars are not intended to be driven without a speedometer, and, folks, neither are we. *Our* speedometer, of course, is the Word of God. The Lord has written us this wonderful love letter to teach us how to drive safely through life. We aren't supposed to judge our pace or lifestyle on the basis of what's going on around us. We aren't supposed to listen to the world's ideas for success, happiness, and fulfillment. We are to listen to God and allow His words to be our guide.

Romans 12:2 says, "Do not be conformed any longer to the pattern of this world, but be transformed by the renewing of your mind." I'll admit, sometimes I have a tendency to listen to the world's wooings and pace myself according to what is going on around me. And the scary part is, for those who don't know the Lord, that's their only point of reference.

When we listen to the world's voice rather than to God's voice, when we pace ourselves according to the culture around us, chances are a Patrolman (the Holy Spirit) will pull us over and hand us a ticket. We shouldn't be surprised when we see that big blue light in our rearview mirror.

The good news is, no matter how many times the Holy Spirit has to pull us over or stop us in our tracks, no matter how many times we fail, the wedding is still going to take place. The Scripture says we are the bride of Christ. One day He will come to take us to the home that He has prepared for us, and there's nothing that will stand in His way.

EIGHT

Our Own Voice

MARY ELIZABETH WAS STROLLING DOWN the cookie aisle at Wal-Mart with her three-year-old daughter, Sarah, riding comfortably in the "front seat" of the buggy. Suddenly, Sarah spied a box of sugar cookies, coated with pink icing and decorated with multicolored sprinkles.

Her eyes brightened with enthusiasm as she put on her best cherub face. "Mommy, I *want* those cookies."

"Oh, Sarah," replied her mom, "we don't need any cookies today. We have plenty at home. Maybe another time."

Ten minutes later, as Mary Elizabeth passed through the checkout line, Sarah tried again. "Mommy, I *need* those cookies."

"No, Sarah, you don't need those cookies. We have plenty at home, and I'm not buying cookies today."

Finally, as they pulled out of the Wal-Mart parking lot, Sarah gave it one last try. "Mommy, I think *God wants me to have* those cookies."

Cissy, Sarah's grandmother, laughed when she told me this story. I laughed too. It was a nervous laugh. For just a moment, I saw myself riding through life in a shopping buggy, pointing at first one thing and then another whining, "I want...I need...God wants me to have."

Sarah already had learned our mechanism for justifying our whims. Whether it's sugar cookies with sprinkles on top or a new red convertible, we mere mortals, given enough time, follow that same progression. For Sarah, she went from *I want* to *I need* to *God wants me to have* in a matter of minutes. For us, it may take a little longer, but the tendency is still there.[1]

In becoming women who listen to God, we must be able to determine if the voice we are hearing is God's voice or our own. We can be easily swayed to rationalize, as Sarah did, to convince ourselves that our fleshly desires are God's desires.

First, let's define the word "flesh" as it is used in the Bible. The Greek word, *sarx*, is translated "flesh" in the NASB and "sinful nature" in the NIV. It is not the flesh and bones of our physical bodies, but the sinful nature we are born with. The flesh tells us to do what *we* want, when *we* want, how *we* want, and places ourselves on the throne of our lives.

When we become a Christian, the Bible says that we are "born again." (See John 3:5-7.) Because of man's disobedience in the Garden of Eden, each of us is born with a dead spirit. At conversion, God breathes life into our spirits and we become a new creation (2 Corinthians 5:17). There are three words for "life" in the Greek: *bios*—life of the body, *psyche*—life of the soul, and *zoe*—life of the Spirit. The word for life that is used in John 3:16 is *zoe*—life of the spirit. "For God so loved the world that he gave his one and only Son, that whoever believes in him shall not perish but have eternal *zoe*" (John 3:16). Our spirits come alive when we accept Christ as our personal Savior. That's what Jesus meant when He told Nicodemus that he must be "born again" to see the kingdom of God. (See John 3:3.)

While we experience a "spiritual makeover" the moment we say, "I believe," our "ultimate makeover," as I refer to it in my book *Ultimate Makeover,* continues for the rest of our lives. At the core of our being, in our spirits, we are a new creation, but on our soulish and physical levels, we still struggle to be conformed to the image of Christ (Romans 8:23). Until we leave this earth by death or meeting Jesus in the air, the old voices of the sinful appetites, attitudes, and habits will cry out to pull us away from Christ. However, as we continue to grow in our relationship with Christ, we will be tuned in to His voice rather than our own.

The longer I am married to Steve, the more we begin to think alike and speak alike and act alike. My dear friend Lysa and I can complete each other's sentences and know what each other is thinking without uttering a word. When Peter denied Jesus the third time after His arrest, the servant girl said she recognized him by the way he talked! (Matthew 26:73 NASB).

Paul has this to say about the contrast between life in the Spirit and life in the flesh,

> Walk by the Spirit, and you will not carry out the desire of the flesh. For the flesh sets its desire against the Spirit, and the Spirit against the flesh; for these are in opposition to one another, so that you may not do the things that you please…Now the deeds of the flesh are evident, which are: immorality, impurity, sensuality, idolatry, sorcery, enmities, strife, jealousy, outbursts of anger, disputes, dissensions, factions, envying, drunkenness, carousing, and things like these, of which I forewarn you just as I have forewarned you that those who practice such things shall not inherit the kingdom of God (Galatians 5:16-21 NASB).

After painting a portrait of life in the flesh, Paul gives us a picture of life in the Spirit. "But the fruit of the Spirit is love, joy, peace, patience, kindness, goodness, faithfulness, gentleness, self-control; against such things there is no law. Now those who belong to Christ Jesus have crucified the flesh with its passions and desires. If we live by the Spirit, let us also walk by the Spirit" (Galatians 5:22-25 NASB).

Paul was no stranger to this struggle of listening to the Spirit over the flesh. "I do not understand what I do," he lamented. "For what I want to do I do not do, but what I hate I do...What a wretched man I am!" (Romans 7:15,24).

Paul was in quite a predicament. He felt wretched. I've been there right along with him. Haven't you? As long as we are listening to the voice of the flesh, dear sisters, we will feel wretched most of the time. Theologians for centuries have argued whether Paul was writing about his life before or after his conversion. I can see arguments for both sides. While that may remain unclear, one thing is certain—Paul was a man struggling to listen to the voice of the Spirit over the voice of the flesh.

Paul uses at least 32 personal pronouns when describing his struggle to make his walk match his talk. That's a lot of "me, myself, and I!" Therein lies the problem! When we focus on our own strengths and abilities, apart from Christ, we will always come up lacking. When we listen to the voice of the flesh instead of the Holy Spirit living in us, we will always feel wretched.

Paul understood the problem, and he also understood the solution. He was so excited to tell us the answer, he couldn't even wait until Romans chapter 8 but blurted it out at the end of Romans 7. "Who will rescue me from this body of death? Thanks be to God—through Jesus Christ our Lord!" (Romans 7:24-25).

Mixed Messages

My friend Katherine and I set out for a lazy summer stroll around the neighborhood just before dusk when the fireflies start to flicker. We chatted about children, husbands, school, and decorating. When we arrived back at her house, she invited me in to look at some fabric swatches for her new sofa. Before I knew it, it was almost 10:00.

"I've been gone for over two hours! I bet Steve's worried sick. He doesn't even know where I am. I'd better give him a call before I start back home."

I dialed the number and the answering machine picked up. After listening to my sweet Southern salutation, I left a not-so-sweet message.

"Steve, I was calling to let you know I'm at Katherine's. I thought you'd be worried, but apparently you don't even care because you won't pick up the phone!" Click. I said my goodbyes and left feeling somewhat dejected as I walked down the dark street to my house.

But who should I meet along the way but Sir Galahad, riding his bike in the dark.

"Where have you been?" he asked. "I've been riding all over the neighborhood looking for you!"

"So you do care," I said with a grin, giving him a big hug.

"What are you talking about?" he asked.

"Oh, nothing. Let's go home." I answered.

When we got back home, I quickly erased the message on the machine before Steve could hear my reprimanding words. *Whew,* I thought, *that was close.*

A few weeks later, Steve called me from work.

"Sharon, have you listened to the answering machine lately?"

"No, why?"

"Well, I think there's something on there you need to hear."

We hung up and I reached for my cell phone to call myself. The message on the answering machine went something like this.

(The voice of a sweet Southern belle) "Hello, you've reached the Jaynes' residence. We're unable to answer the phone right now...(enter the voice of Cruella DeVille) I was calling to let you know I'm at Katherine's. I thought you'd be worried, but apparently you don't even care because you won't pick up the phone! (Return of sweet Southern belle) At the sound of the beep, leave your number and we'll get back with you as soon as possible." Beep.

"Oh my goodness!" I screamed. "How did this happen! How many people have heard this over the past two weeks?"

I called the phone company, and they explained that sometimes during a thunderstorm, lightning strikes the wires and
answering machine messages get scrambled. The message
somehow got attached to the greeting.

I was mortified. It sounded like Dr. Jekyll and Mrs. Hyde rein-
carnate.

"Lord," I prayed. "This is so embarrassing."

"Yes, it is," He replied.

Well, He didn't really *say* that in so many words. It was more
like this. "With the tongue we praise our Lord and Father, and with
it we curse men, who have been made in God's likeness. Out of
the same mouth come praise and cursing. My brothers, this should
not be. Can both fresh water and salt water flow from the same
spring? My brothers, can a fig tree bear olives, or a grapevine bear
figs? Neither can a salt spring produce fresh water" (James 3:9-12).

"Okay, Lord, I got the message." I prayed. But unfortunately, so
did a lot of other people.

Carnal Clattering

Society continuously appeals to our fleshly desires through
television commercials, magazine ads, and highway billboards.
Have you ever seen an electric razor commercial with a frumpy,
overweight balding man gliding the razor across his stubby face?
On the contrary, we see a well-chiseled, lean, bare-chested 20-
something bodybuilder moving the razor romantically over his
tanned cheek. What are they appealing to? You tell me. We live in
a world filled with carnal clattering, which can drown out the still,
small voice of God.

Don't you just love Peter? He was the first to jump out of the
boat and attempt to walk on water, the first to recognize Jesus was
the Christ, the first to defend Jesus and lop off the soldier's ear, the
first to rush into the empty tomb, and the first to jump from his
fishing boat and swim toward his risen Lord. Peter got a lot of
things right, but he also occasionally listened to the wrong voice.

After the disciples had been with Jesus for quite some time, He asked, "'Who do you say I am?' Simon Peter answered, 'You are the Christ, the Son of the living God.' Jesus replied, 'Blessed are you, Simon son of Jonah, for this was not revealed to you by man, but by my Father in heaven. And I tell you that you are Peter, and on this rock I will build my church, and the gates of Hades will not overcome it.'" (Matthew 16:15-18). Peter must have been feeling pretty good about himself about then, wouldn't you say? Yes, he was listening and listening well!

But then we scan down a few verses where Jesus was telling His disciples about His imminent death and resurrection. "Peter took him aside and began to rebuke him. 'Never, Lord!' he said. 'This shall never happen to you!' Jesus turned and said to Peter, 'Get behind me, Satan! You are a stumbling block to me; you do not have in mind the things of God, but the things of men'" (Matthew 16:22-23). Oh my! Call me wrong, but don't call me Satan. The Peter who heard God clearly in verse 16 did not hear God at all in verse 22. He went from being a building block to being a stumbling block in a matter of moments.

As we become women who listen to God, let's not become discouraged if sometimes we "don't get it right." Even precious Peter made a few mistakes, so we're in good company.

The only way to distinguish between our own voice and God's voice is...you guessed it...by developing a personal, ongoing, intimate relationship with Jesus Christ and knowing the truth of God's Word.

- ❧ The flesh says look out for yourself because no one else will.

- ❧ God's voice says love others more than yourself and think of their interests above your own. (Philippians 2:3-4)

- ❧ The flesh says get your own way.

- ❧ God's voice says be a peacemaker. (Romans 12:18)

- ❧ The flesh says get even.
- ❧ God's voice says forgive. (Matthew 18:21)

- ❧ The flesh says glorify self.
- ❧ God's voice says glorify Christ. (John 17:5)

- ❧ The flesh says quit.
- ❧ God's voice says be committed. (Matthew 5:37)

- ❧ The flesh calls for instant gratification.
- ❧ God's voice says exercise self-control. (Galatians 5:23)

- ❧ The flesh calls for pride.
- ❧ God's voice calls for humility. (Philippians 2:3)

- ❧ The flesh says look good on the outside and no one will notice the ugliness on the inside.
- ❧ God's voice says be pure on the inside and the outside won't even matter. (Proverbs 31:30)

Mirage

Flutter. Flutter. Bang! Flutter. Flutter. Bang! Mama and Papa Bluebird danced in front of our sunroom windows, trying frantically to break through the glass barrier. Time and time again they banged their feathered heads against the panes. What were they pursuing? Where were they trying to go? What had caught their eye? Why were they so persistent? I wanted desperately to help them solve their dilemma, but I couldn't figure out what the dilemma was.

After three days of this featherbrained, frenzied activity, I decided to put myself in their position, get a bird's-eye view, and examine the situation from their perspective. I stepped out onto the patio, stood in front of the windows, and there it was. In the reflection of the glass was mirrored their birdhouse, some 30 feet behind me.

Mr. and Mrs. Bluebird's lovely cedar shingled home with decorative finial sat on a tall pole nestled under the protective branches of an old oak tree. Their bed-and-breakfast came equipped with an adjoining spa—a concrete birdbath surrounded by fragrant rose bushes bursting with red blossoms and a carpet of white annuals. But instead of being satisfied with their high-rise estate, they were banging their heads against the windowpane, striving for a mirage, a mere reflection.

Amazingly, a few times they turned around, soared to their home, and crept through its opening for a reprieve. But before long, they were dive bombing into the glass again, trying to gain entrance into an illusion.

This made me think of my own life and the many times I go flutter, flutter, bang—flutter, flutter, bang, striving for something that is just a cheap imitation of God's perfect provision for my life. Jeremiah 29:11 says, "For I know the plans I have for you, plans to prosper you and not to harm you, plans to give you hope and a future."

And yet I argue, "Yeah, I know that, God. I know You've provided me with this home and this job and with these particular gifts. But, well, I don't mean to sound ungrateful or anything, but I really would be happy if You'd give me a house like Mary's over there. And You know Beth? Well, I really would be happy if you made me a Bible teacher like she is. And You know Teresa? If I could just be as sweet as she is, I'd be satisfied. Then there's Laura. Now, God, she has the prettiest and silkiest blonde hair. Could I just have hair like hers? Don't get me wrong, Lord. I do appreciate what You have given me, but if I could just have…"

Well, you get the picture.

Flutter. Flutter. Bang! Flutter. Flutter. Bang!

The banging birds may have knocked themselves silly, but they also knocked some sense into my hard head. God has provided me with everything I need. As David, the psalmist wrote, the Lord is my Shepherd, I don't need anything! I can flutter about looking at the mirage of happiness in other people's windows, or I can nestle down in contentment and not get my feathers ruffled trying to get more. The way to keep from fluttering around from one mirage of happiness to the other is to stay close to home and be satisfied with my own nest, feathers, and chicks. I've learned that I'm most content when I'm at home in the Father's will, nestled in His protective branches, perched on the pole of His standard, nurtured by the living water of His fountain, cleansed in the laver of the Holy Spirit, and beautified by the fragrance of the rose of Sharon. As Dorothy of Kansas once said, "There's no place like home."

NINE

The Deceiver's Voice

AFTER MY FIRST TWO YEARS of college, I moved into the upstairs apartment of my parents' home and began work as a dental hygienist. My mother and father both worked long hours, so this arrangement gave me freedom to stretch my wings and pad my savings account.

One night I was getting dressed to go out for the evening. My dad was out of town on business and my mom was at a Wednesday night church service. Just as I was putting the finishing touches on my mascara, I heard a rattling by the bathroom window. Because it was dark outside, I turned off the light to get a better view. When I did, I saw a man in the window, standing on a ladder, staring at me. I froze with fear. Then it was as if the hand of God propelled my body down the stairs, out the front door, and across the street. I was counting on being able to run faster than he could get down from the ladder. As I shot across the yard, I ran right past his car parked by my front curb.

I burst through my neighbor's back door and just stood paralyzed and ashen-faced. Mrs. Scarborough gently shook my shoulders and said, "Sharon, what's wrong?"

After a few seconds I replied, "There's a man at my bathroom window."

Mrs. Scarborough called the police, and they were there in minutes. Amazingly, my mother drove up at the same time.

"Something just told me to come home," she said. "So I got up in the middle of the service and left."

Of course, the perpetrator was long gone by the time the police arrived. The only remains of his presence was the ladder left leaning against the house. This was a frightening experience for me, but the reality of what could have happened hit even harder when we all realized that the upstairs bathroom window was the only window in the entire house that did not have a lock. The upstairs apartment was a later addition, and no one had ever gotten around to putting a lock on the bathroom window. Did he know this was the one unprotected area of our home? I suspect so. You better believe we put a lock on the window that very night. But what a lesson I learned.

The Bible says that Satan is like a roaring lion seeking someone to devour. He looks for the chinks in the armor, the unsecured window, the unlocked door. God told Cain in Genesis 4:7, "Sin is crouching at your door; it desires to have you, but you must master it." He still crouches and looks for windows of opportunity to catch us off guard and whisper tempting thoughts or lies into our ears.

From Genesis to Revelation we see a battle going on for the hearts, minds, and souls of God's children. The antagonist has many names: Satan, the devil, the accuser of the brethren, angel of light, wolf in sheep's clothing, Lucifer, liar, and the father of lies. Satan is also called "the deceiver." A deceiver is someone who presents a lie in such a way that it sounds like the truth. He can make you believe something is not true when it is, and make you believe something is true when it isn't. He speaks to us today in the same way he spoke to Eve in the garden. Oh, we may not have a conversation with a cunning serpent, but he slithers into our lives, nonetheless.

The book of Genesis opens with the beautiful picture of God creating the heavens and the earth, the land and the sea, vegetation, and crawling, flying, and swimming creatures. But something was missing. God longed for someone like Himself with whom to have a relationship, to communicate on an intimate level. So on the sixth day God created man in His own image, male and female He created them. Adam and Eve were perfect in every way. Their bodies had no genetic defects or flaws, their souls were naked and unashamed, and their spirits were in perfect union and communion with God. But in Genesis 3 Satan comes on the scene with the goal of destroying man's utopic world. How does he accomplish his mission? Through lies and deception.

God had placed only one restriction on Adam and Eve. He said,

> I give you every seed-bearing plant on the face of the whole earth and every tree that has fruit with seed in it. They will be yours for food. And to all the beasts of the earth and all the birds of the air and all the creatures that move on the ground—everything that has the breath of life in it—I give every green plant for food (Genesis 1:29-30).

Then God gave the one restriction: "You are free to eat from any tree in the garden; but you must not eat from the tree of the knowledge of good and evil, for when you eat of it you will surely die" (Genesis 2:16-17).

So Satan slithered into the Garden and tempted Eve with the very thing God had forbidden.

1. He questioned God. "Did God really say, 'You must not eat from any tree in the garden'?" (Genesis 3:1)

2. He denied God. "You will not surely die!" the serpent said to the woman. (Genesis 3:4)

3. He questioned God's justice. "For God knows that when you eat of it your eyes will be opened, and you will be like God, knowing good and evil." (Genesis 3:5)

Eve believed the lie over the truth, ate the forbidden fruit, and ushered sin and shame into the world. She and her husband, who also ate the fruit, were banished from the Garden and from God's presence. And while their bodies did not die right away, their spirits died at once.

Dear friends, Satan is not very creative, but he is very effective. He uses the same tactics with us today that he used with Eve in the Garden. Paul wrote, "Do not be ignorant of his (Satan's) schemes" (2 Corinthians 2:11 NASB). We will not be able to defeat the lies of the enemy if we cannot recognize his voice. Just like with Eve, Satan whispers for us to question God. *Did God say that you must stay married to a man who doesn't meet your needs?* He whispers for us to deny God. *God wouldn't count it as a sin for you to seek happiness in the arms of another man.* And he whispers for us to doubt God's justice. *What kind of God is He who would deny you the right to find happiness with a man who appreciates you?* If we believe the lies and taste the forbidden fruit, the result will be the same as Eve's—death. Death to our hopes, our dreams, our peace, and our joy.

There is only one way to recognize Satan's lies—know the truth. When bank tellers are being trained to know the difference between counterfeit and real money, their instructors teach them the difference by using real money. They are taught what authentic money looks like—the coloring, the numbering, the markings—in order to recognize the fake. Likewise, we recognize the enemy's lies by knowing the truth—the Word of God.

In 1 Chronicles 21:1, the writer notes, "Satan rose up against Israel and incited David to take a census of Israel." God had previously told David not to count his men. God wanted David to rely on Him and not on numbers. So wouldn't you know it, that was the very idea Satan put in his head to do. Of course David thought taking a census of his army was his own idea, but the Bible clearly states that it was not. Had David been committed to using God's words as his plumb line, he would not have listened to the deceiver's voice. Instead, he would have recognized it as a trap for disobedience.

In my book *Ultimate Makeover*, I have a formula for defeating the lies of Satan:

- Realize the enemy's true identity. (Satan)
- Recognize Satan's lies. (By knowing the truth)
- Reject the lies.
- Replace the lies with truth.[1]

It's been said that every spiritual battle is won or lost at the threshold of the mind—as soon as the lie approaches the door. Don't let the lie in. Don't entertain the thought. Delete that mental e-mail as quickly as possible.

In the New Testament, we see a scenario similar to Eve's in the Garden. Only this time, Satan chose the wrong person to attempt to deceive. He came to the Truth Himself. Jesus had been praying and fasting in the desert for 40 days. The tempter came to Him with three deceptions, just the way he did with Eve. But Jesus fought him with the only effective weapon available to man—God's Word—the truth—the sword of the spirit (Ephesians 6:17). Each time Satan tempted Jesus to deny God, Jesus quoted Scripture. Satan's goal was to convince Jesus to circumvent the cross and accept a counterfeit plan. His goal for us is to convince us to circumvent God's plan for our lives and accept a counterfeit plan as well.

Author Neil Anderson said this about Satan, "You don't have to outshout him or outmuscle him to be free of his influence. You just have to *outtruth* him."[2]

When Satan speaks to us, like David, we may not recognize his voice. He's crafty, oh, he's crafty. One reason is because he speaks to us in our own voice and uses first person pronouns. He doesn't say, "You are so stupid." He whispers in your ear and causes you to think, "I am so stupid." He speaks in your voice and with your accent. It sounds like you and feels like you, so you think it is you. Satan is not omnipotent (all-powerful) or omniscient (all-knowing), and while he cannot read your mind, he does memorize your habit patterns, weaknesses, and chinks in your armor. He knows exactly where you struggle and will attempt to destroy you in those very areas. That is why it is imperative that we recognize his voice.

For many years I lived my Christian life bound by feelings of inferiority, insecurity, and inadequacy. Why? Because I was listening to the wrong voice. I listened to lies of Satan that said, "God may love you, but He sure couldn't possibly like you," "The Bible works for other people, but it won't work for you," "If you were a better Christian, you'd spend more time in prayer," "If you had more faith, you'd see more miracles," "If God really loved you, He'd answer your prayer to have more children." On and on the lies played in my head, like old sitcom reruns—only they weren't funny.

It wasn't until I began to see the truth of who I was in Christ, what I had in Christ, and where I was in Christ, that I could recognize the lies, defeat the enemy, and start living as a child of the King instead of a pauper begging for handouts.

"The thief comes only to steal and kill and destroy," Jesus said, "I have come that they may have life, and have it to the full" (John 10:10). Learning to discern between Satan's voice and God's can mean the difference between a life that is empty and a life that is abundantly full. The only way to distinguish between Satan's voice and God's voice is...you guessed it...by developing a personal, ongoing, intimate relationship with Jesus Christ and knowing the truth of God's Word.

- Satan says you could never succeed.
- God's voice says you can do everything through Him who gives you strength. (Philippians 4:13)

- Satan says nobody loves you.
- God says He loves you so much He sacrificed His only Son for you. (John 3:16)

- Satan says you're no match for him.
- God says greater is He that is in you (Jesus) than he that is in the world. (1 John 4:4)

- Satan says you're damaged goods.
- God says you are a new creation in Christ. (2 Corinthians 5:17)

- Satan says nobody likes you.
- God calls you His friend. (John 15:15)

- Satan says you should be ashamed of yourself.
- God says there is now no condemnation for those who are in Christ Jesus. (Romans 8:1)

- Satan says if it feels good, do it.
- God says be controlled by the Spirit. (Romans 8:6)

- Satan says that's just the way you are.
- God says your old self was crucified with Christ and you are no longer a slave to sin. (Romans 6:6)

Nightmare on York Street

One night when I was 13, I lay in my bed unmoving, wide-eyed, and paralyzed by fear after watching a scary movie with my dad. The silence was interrupted only by the sound of my heart drumming in my ears. The movie, *In Cold Blood,* was about two murderous maniacs and their race from the law. A trail of heinous crimes littered the screen as the crazed men traversed the countryside. By today's standards, this movie would be considered mild. But to this 13-year-old girl, it was the scariest thing I had ever seen.

So one hour after the credits rolled, I lay quivering in my bed with the covers clinched tightly against my chin, fully expecting the two killers to make my house at 725 York Street their next stop. The fact that my dad was asleep in the next room was no comfort or consolation.

At some point my mother made her way to their room. I heard her open their bedroom door. I heard her steps as she walked toward their bed. Then suddenly I heard a man let out a bloodcurdling scream, "Aaaaaaaaahhhhhhh!" and what sounded like my mother being thrown against the wall with a thud.

"Get out! Get out!" she shrieked.

I bolted upright in the bed and knew I had to escape before the killers made their way to my room. Straining to open the window, I managed to push it up and jump out onto the wet grass. Getting to my feet, I tried to run toward my neighbor's house. My mind was racing faster than my shaking legs, and several times I tumbled to the ground. As if in slow motion, I ran, tripped, and crawled to Mrs. Dixon's house.

Bam! Bam! Bam! I rapped on the wooden door.

No answer.

Bam! Bam! Bam!

The household awoke as lights sprang to life. Mrs. Dixon cautiously cracked the door to find a trembling teenager with a mixture of white night cream and mud smeared on her face, hair pulled up in a rubber band and wound around one gargantuan curler, bare wet feet, and tattered pajamas.

"My goodness, Sharon. What has happened to you?" she exclaimed as the pulled me in out of the cold.

Between sobs, I described the scene. (In graphic detail, I might add.)

"There's a bloodthirsty murderer in my house. He has already killed my father, and now he's killing my mom! I jumped out the window to escape! You've got to help us!" I pleaded as I grabbed at her robe.

By now, the entire Dixon household was awake and gathered in the den. Included in my audience was the handsome son, five years my senior, whom I was always desiring to impress. Before notifying the police, Mrs. Dixon decided to call my home. Surprisingly, my mom answered.

"Louise, this is Margarite. Sharon is over here and says someone's trying to kill you. Are you all right?"

My mom, who had no idea I had fled the premises, explained, "There's no problem over here. Allan had watched a scary movie on TV. He was having a nightmare that a murderer was coming after him. Right when I crawled into bed, he was dreaming the bogeyman was grabbing his shoulder. Allan jumped up and pushed me against the wall."

Listening in on my mom's response, I pleaded. "She's not telling the truth! He's making her say that. He's killed my father and he's holding her hostage. I heard her yell, 'Get out! Get out!'"

"No," Mom assured Mrs. Dixon, "I yelled, 'Get the light! Get the light!'"

Somehow, Mom convinced the Dixons that no crime had been committed and it was safe for me to come home. Reluctantly, I made my way back across the yard (accompanied by the son, whom I can safely say had been duly impressed). My mother was fine. However, my dad was looking through all the closets in the house with a flashlight.

I've never enjoyed scary movies since and have concluded that being terrified out of my mind is not my idea of entertainment. And even though it may not have been real, it sure did feel that way.

Here's a little acronym I remember for the word "fear." False Evidence Appearing Real.

Yes, there is a real bogeyman. His name is Satan, or the devil, and he seeks to kill, steal, and destroy. His weapon? Lies. He whispers lies. He wants us to worry about things that are not real. He desires to steal our peace, rob our joy, stir up doubt, and distort what we hear. He twists the truth and plunders our thoughts. His goal is to make us jump, run, or be paralyzed into inactivity.

Oh, he's real, all right. But his lies are not. It's just false evidence appearing real. I suggest you do a little FBI work (Further Bible Investigation). Dust for fingerprints on the worries of your life. I bet they indicate Satan's been all over them.

By the way, he's already been arrested and convicted. Right now he's out on parole. But this is one movie where I've already seen the ending. He gets his due. The list of credits is short—there's only one name—Jesus.

Take Every Thought Captive

It was my first experience at a cowboy rodeo. There we sat, three city slickers among whoopin', hollerin' locals at the Saturday night rodeo in Jackson Hole, Wyoming. It wasn't hard to tell the tourists from the locals. There were Reeboks among cowboy boots, scarves among bandannas, chewing gum among chewing tobacco, baseball caps among ten-gallon, wide-brim hats, and skimpy nylon windbreakers among warm fringed suede jackets. (Who knew that temperatures on a July night would plummet to 35 degrees when the sun set behind the Grand Tetons?)

The cowboys' skills entertained and amazed those of us who thought a bronco was a four-wheel-drive. Cowboys, young and old, mastered mustangs, raced around barrels, and conquered angry bulls. But the most thrilling event was the lassoing contest.

The announcer introduced, "And now here's the Jackson Hole High School Lassoing champion for 1997."

My son looked at me in amazement. "They have lassoing as a school sport? They do this in PE? Well, I guess they don't have a golf team."

We all sat on the edge of our seats as the cowboy waited, poised in his saddle, anticipating the calf's release from the chute. The corral door swung open and the calf burst from the gate. The cowboy, with lasso in hand, went after the bucking, twisting, galloping animal, lassoed his neck, threw him to the ground, quickly wrapped the rope around his legs, tied them securely in place, and immediately jumped up and raised his arms in victory. As the victor stood receiving his applause, his trained steed took three steps backward to secure the rope in place. "Yup, that little heifer ain't goin' nowhere," the horse seemed to say.

The timer continued to run for a few seconds to make sure the calf was indeed captive. Then the cowboy's time was posted on the scoreboard.

Time and time again, cowhands lassoed little calves, secured their captives, and raised their hands in victory. Only a few times did a calf escape the rope and make his exit through the door on the other end.

I'll admit that I was feeling a bit sorry for the little calves, even though they were released as soon as the time was logged. But the Lord began to do a little whoopin' and hollerin' of His own and told me to pay attention to what was happenin'.

As I watched ropin' after ropin', God began to reveal to me that this was a perfect picture of what Paul described in 2 Corinthians 10:5. "We are destroying speculations and every lofty thing raised up against the knowledge of God, and we are *taking every thought captive* to the obedience of Christ" (NASB).

I began to see those calves as the wild and woolly thoughts that burst forth from the stable of my mind at times: negative, rebellious, fearful, angry, worrisome, jealous thoughts that are untamed and unruly, bucking, jumping, and running wild across pleasant plains. And God showed me that my reaction should be that of the cowboy: ride up hot on the thought's heels, lasso it, tie it up, and throw it back in the dust where it came from. My response should be just like the cowboy's trusty trained horse who, automatically, because of practice, takes three steps backward to make sure the negative thought "ain't goin' nowhere."

Trained because of practice. Taking every thought captive—whether from the world, the flesh, or the devil. Yes, siree. Let's lasso those thoughts, little sister, tie 'em up, and throw 'em back in the dust where they came from in the first place. It was a verse I had been pondering, and now the Lord had made it crystal clear.

Taking every thought captive to the obedience of Christ may take a lot of lassoing and practice, but in the end, we can join the rodeo cowboy, raise our arms in victory, and listen for the applause of heaven.

PART III

Barriers to Hearing
God's Voice

CAN YOU HEAR ME NOW?

When my son, Steven, was 13 years old, he was appalled at my lack of technological advancement in the area of communication. It was during a time in the 1990s when it seemed everyone was getting a cell phone except his mom. I didn't want a cell phone so I could be reached at anytime, anyplace, by anyone. My chariot (a silver-blue station wagon) served as a quiet place of escape as I scurried around from place to place. *Why would I want to be interrupted by the constant ringing?* I thought.

But Steven's insistence continued regardless of my indifference to modern technology.

"Mom, why don't you have a cell phone?" he asked one day on the way to school. "Everybody else has one."

"Everyone?" I asked. "Your dad doesn't have one."

"Okay, Dad doesn't, but tell me another mom, besides Grandma, who doesn't," he argued.

Actually, his grandmother did have one, but I didn't think this was the time to share that information with him. "Son," I explained, "I just don't need a cell phone. I like getting in my car and listening to the quiet, and I don't want to be accessible 24 hours a day. Besides, 'everyone else has one' has never been much of a motivator for me."

"But Mom, when you're driving me to school in the mornings and the radio DJ does those Bible trivia questions, I know a lot of the answers! If we had a phone, I could call in and win all sorts of CDs and concert tickets!"

Steven knew just which strings to pull, but I held my ground.

"I don't need a cell phone, and being able to call the radio station to win prizes is not a good reason to pay monthly service fees. End of subject."

Boy, was I surprised the following Christmas when I opened up my present from Steven to find a flip-top mobile phone, purchased with his own money. Steven had convinced my husband that our town was no longer a safe place for a woman to be driving around in without a cell phone. Suppose I ran out of gas? Suppose I was in an accident? Suppose I was hijacked, for goodness' sake? Steven had agreed to pay $10 for the phone if Steve agreed to pay the monthly service fees. My husband bought it hook, line, and sinker from that 13-year-old stinker.

I opened the box, pulled out the phone, and looked up at Steven, who was grinning like a Cheshire cat who had eaten the pet canary.

"Oh, thank you, Steven," I said, "Now when Dad and I are out and you are home alone, I can call you anytime and from anyplace to see what you are doing. How thoughtful of you."

From the look on his face, a canary bone suddenly lodged in his throat. Obviously, the thought of me being able to check up on him had not crossed his mind.

A few weeks later, I decided to try out my new toy. Steve and I had gone out for the evening and were on our way home, so I called Steven.

"Steven, this is Mom. Dad and I are in the car and I want to try out the phone. When I hang up, you call me and let's see how it works."

"Okay," he said.

We waited a few minutes, but the phone never rang. I called Steven back to see what the problem was.

"Steven, this is Mom again. What happened?"

"I called your number," he explained, "but the operator said either your phone wasn't turned on or you were out of range."

"That can't be right. The phone is definitely on and I'm only a few miles from home. Try again."

Steven tried again, but with the same results. The call would not go through.

The next day, I called the cell phone company to find out why I was having trouble receiving calls.

"Mrs. Jaynes, where were you when you tried to receive the call?" the service operator asked.

"I was on Randolph Road near Central Church," I answered.

"Let me explain how this works," she said. "A cellular phone works by sending out and receiving radio waves from a cell site tower. You were at a point on Randolph Road that dips down into a small valley and the radio waves could not reach down into the dip for you to receive the signals.

"Another possibility," she continued, "was that the large church there was blocking the signal. We have trouble uptown with large buildings blocking the radio transmissions all the time.

"And, Mrs. Jaynes, was your battery powered up?"

"Yes, I had just charged it up that morning. It was fully charged."

"How about the antenna? Was the antenna up?" she asked.

"No, the antenna wasn't up, but I hadn't planned on walking around town with my antenna sticking out of my pocketbook."

"That might have been a problem as well."

"Let me get this straight," I said, summing up the conversation. "In order for this new piece of technological wonder to work properly, I cannot be in a dip in the road or behind a tall building, and I must have the battery fully charged and the antenna up. Is that correct?"

"That's pretty much it," she replied.

"One more question," I continued. "Why is it that I could place a call, but I had trouble receiving a call?"

"That's because it takes more cell strength to receive a call than to send a call," she replied.

I was more than frustrated with this 2 x 6 piece of plastic and power cells and failed to see the draw of owning one. Then I settled down to spend my daily quiet time with the Lord. I was trying to calm my spirit when God sent a call...

Could the reasons you had difficulty receiving a transmission on your cell phone be the same reasons you have difficulty receiving a transmission from Me? Could those be the same reasons you have trouble hearing My voice?

That came through loud and clear, and for the next several days I studied, prayed, listened, and came to realize the similarities for poor reception on both accounts are remarkable. Join me now as we take a look at five reasons we might have poor reception when it comes to hearing God's voice and becoming a woman who listens to God.

TEN

Low Dips of Emotion

THE FIRST QUESTION THE OPERATOR ASKED was about my location. I was in a dip in the road—a depression or valley that did not allow the radio waves to reach my cell phone. Likewise, when I'm not hearing God's voice, I have to ask myself the same question. Where am I? Am I in an emotional dip in the road, down in the dumps or suffering from a bad case of the blues? Am I depressed or despairing? At times like those, I often cry out, "God where are You? I can't hear You. Are You there?"

As I read through the psalms, I noticed many times King David felt the same way. David was anointed to be the next king of Israel when he was just a young shepherd boy, and this did not sit well with Saul, the present king. For many years King Saul and his army tried to kill David. David hid in caves, lived on the run, and even masqueraded as a lunatic. While there were probably many days David was unsure of God's plan, he was never unsure of God's character. During this time, he wrote many of his psalms. In quite a few, he began by singing the blues, but after recounting the unfailing character of God, he concluded by singing songs of praise.

"Answer me when I call to you, O my righteous God. Give me relief from my distress; be merciful to me and hear my prayer" (Psalm 4:1). David was distressed, but then he began praising God and ended the psalm reassured. "I will lie down and sleep in peace, for you alone, O Lord, make me dwell in safety" (Psalm 4:8).

David began Psalm 13, "How long, O Lord? Will you forget me, forever? How long will you hide your face from me?" He was definitely in a dip in the road and having difficulty hearing from the Lord. Then he began praising God and ended the psalm with "I will sing to the Lord, for he has been good to me" (Psalm 13:6).

Again, in Psalm 64, David began in the pit of despair but ended on the pinnacle of praise. "Hear me, O God, as I voice my complaint; protect my life from the threat of the enemy" (Psalm 64:1). Then once again he begins to praise God, and the Lord lifts him out of the pit. This is how he ends what began as a lament: "Let the righteous rejoice in the Lord and take refuge in him; let all the upright in heart praise him!" (64:10).

Let me give you an example. One day mopping the kitchen floor had me in a less-than-cheerful mood. Then God began to whisper a new thought to my heart. *Suppose you were blind and couldn't see the beautiful patterns on the linoleum floor, or the spilled juice by the refrigerator, or the crumbs under the baby's chair? If you were deaf, you couldn't hear the soothing sound of the soap bubbles dissolving in the scrub bucket. You couldn't hear the rhythmic sound of the mop being pushed back and forth across the floor's hard surface. Suppose you were confined to a wheelchair and not strong enough to stand upright and grasp the wooden handle to erase the muddy footprints and make the floor shiny and clean again? Suppose you didn't have a home or a family to clean up after?*

These thoughts brought a new perspective to this mundane task, and my grumblings turned into a prayer of thanksgiving. I stood up straight, proudly grasped the mop, and began to pray. *Thank You, Lord, for the privilege of mopping this dirty floor. Thank*

You for the health and strength to hold this mop, for the ability to wrap my agile fingers around its handle and feel the wood in my hands. Thank You for the sight to see the crumbs and the dirt, for the sense of smell to enjoy the clean scent of the soap in my bucket. Thank You for the precious feet that will walk through this room and dirty it again. Those feet are the reason I do this job. And Lord, thank You for the privilege of having a floor to mop and a family to clean up after.

Ah yes, the difference a godly perspective can have on our ability to listen to God. Psalm 77 is a wonderful example of a man having difficulty hearing from God because he was despairing and how, through praising God and remembering His blessings, he returned to level ground. It is David's own version of *Thank You, Lord, for My Dirty Floor.*

> I cried out to God for help;
> I cried out to God to hear me.
> When I was in distress, I sought the Lord;
> at night I stretched out untiring hands
> and my soul refused to be comforted.
> I remembered you, O God, and I groaned;
> I mused, and my spirit grew faint.
> *Selah*
>
> You kept my eyes from closing;
> I was too troubled to speak.
> I thought about the former days,
> the years of long ago;
> I remembered my songs in the night.
> My heart mused and my spirit inquired:
> "Will the Lord reject forever?
> Will he never show his favor again?
> Has his unfailing love vanished forever?
> Has his promise failed for all time?
> Has God forgotten to be merciful?

Has he in anger withheld his compassion?"
Selah

Then I thought, "To this I will appeal:
the years of the right hand of the Most High."
I will remember the deeds of the LORD;
yes, I will remember your miracles of long ago.
I will meditate on all your works
and consider all your mighty deeds.
Your ways, O God, are holy.
What god is so great as our God?
You are the God who performs miracles;
you display your power among the peoples.
With your mighty arm you redeemed your people,
the descendants of Jacob and Joseph.
Selah

The waters saw you, O God,
the waters saw you and writhed;
the very depths were convulsed.
The clouds poured down water,
the skies resounded with thunder;
your arrows flashed back and forth.
Your thunder was heard in the whirlwind,
your lightning lit up the world;
the earth trembled and quaked.
Your path led through the sea,
your way through the mighty waters,
though your footprints were not seen.
You led your people like a flock
by the hand of Moses and Aaron.

Did you notice when David's emotions began to crawl out of the pit? As soon as he began to praise the Lord, his emotions began to creep back up to level ground and eventually to the mountaintop of praise.

How do we get out of the dip in the road in order to improve our "reception?" Begin by praising God. Put praise music on the CD player. Pop a worshipful cassette tape in the car stereo. Make a list of reasons to be thankful. Visit a homeless shelter. He inhabits the praises of His people! Praise God for who He is and for what He has done in your life. Praise Him for His beautiful creation. Praise Him for His almighty power, wisdom, and might. As the old hymn says, "Count your blessings, name them one by one. Count your blessings, see what God has done." Sure, there may be times when we simply don't *feel* like praising God. That's when we offer up a *sacrifice* of praise.

"I waited patiently for the LORD; he turned to me and heard my cry. He lifted me out of the slimy pit, out of the mud and mire; he set my feet on a rock and gave me a firm place to stand" (Psalm 40:1-2). And where will that rock be situated? It will not be in a valley with poor reception, but on a holy hill (Psalm 15:1)!

Something to Smile About

It was a tense drive to school on a crisp December morning. I don't know which had the greater chill—the morning air at 6:30 A.M. or our attitudes. My son and I were not speaking. Just a few months before, he had transferred from a school of 489 students to a school of 2500. While his social life was thriving in the new and exciting environment filled with diversity, diversions, and distractions, his grades were on the decline. Our drives to school were usually chatty, but not today. I was tired. He was frustrated. I was disappointed. He was sullen.

I had already met with the advanced placement chemistry and advanced placement English teachers. Today it was Mrs. Morris in Spanish 3. As we pulled up to the visitors' parking lot, the security guard stopped me.

"Sorry, ma'am," he said. "You can't park in this lot in the mornings."

"But this is where I was told to park. I've got an appointment with a teacher." I explained.

"Well, this is where the busses for the handicapped kids unload in the mornings. I'll let you park in here today, but from now on, drive around to the other side of the school."

"Thanks," I said as I rolled my window back up. "I like this school less and less," I grumbled to myself.

Steven just cut his eyes over my way as if to say, "Oh, brother."

I met with Mrs. Morris, and we played with the numbers, she offered suggestions, and we made predictions. I guess I was supposed to feel encouraged, but I didn't.

When I went back out to my car, there was a bit more activity stirring around campus as busses filed in from every direction. Kids dressed in baggy jeans and clunky shoes with ten-ton backpacks slung over their shoulders brushed past me rushing to make their first-period class. The cold air hit me in the face as I exited the building. I slid into my seat, turned on the ignition, and backed out of my parking space. As I headed toward the entrance, the same security guard blew his whistle and held up his hand for me to stop.

"What does he want now?" I huffed.

I turned my head to the left and discovered the reason for my delay. A bus filled with handicapped teens was unloading. All I could do was wait—and watch.

He was about 15 years old, I guess. It was hard to tell because of the frailness of his frame. He wore thick glasses, a worn, tattered jacket, and a woolen cap on his head. His limbs twitched spasmodically as he tried to propel his body forward, clinging to the doors of the bus in an attempt to steady his steps. Three sunny adults waited to greet him and welcome him to another day of life. One woman held his arms to guide him down the two steps. Another simultaneously placed a helmet on his head and fastened the strap under his chin. A third woman held a walker steady until he could get a firm grasp on the cold steel handles. Then he grinned at the threesome, proud of his accomplishment.

At that moment, God seemed to say to me, "Sharon, look at those teachers' faces. What do you see?"

"They're smiling, Lord."

"Look at that boy's face. What do you see?"

"He's smiling, Lord."

"Now, My child, look at your face in the mirror. What do you see?"

The security guard walked over to my car and thumped on the hood to startle me out of my daze. "You can go now, ma'am."

I drove out of the parking lot, barely able to drive because of the tears streaming down my cheeks. For weeks I had been unhappy because of my son's lack of achievement in school. And then God sent one of His precious angels to remind me of my many blessings and how I took those blessings for granted.

When my husband came home from work, he asked, "How was the teacher conference?"

"Oh, it was fine," I said, smiling happily. "But let me tell you about the one I had with God in the parking lot."

ELEVEN

Tall Walls of Sin

THE SECOND POSSIBILITY of my not being able to receive a call on my cell phone was that the tall church building was blocking the signal. Sometimes in our spiritual lives, we can erect walls that block God's voice. Walls of pride, selfish ambition, materialism, hard-heartedness, bitterness, and rebellion—just to name a few. Remember the particular wall that was blocking my reception? It was a church building. Yes, even religion can get in the way of a personal relationship with God. In the Bible, some of those who refused to listen to God's voice were religious leaders: Pharisees, Sadducees, and priests.

While there are many walls that interfere with our ability to hear God's voice, perhaps the most common is sin and the refusal to repent. David wrote, "Behold, the LORD's hand is not so short that it cannot save, nor is His ear so dull that it cannot hear. But your iniquities have made a *separation* between you and your God, and your sins have hidden His face from you so that He does not hear" (Isaiah 59:1-2 NASB, emphasis added).

We all sin everyday, but the wall of sin I'm speaking of here is a habitual sin or stronghold of sin we refuse to remove or tear down. We build this wall brick by brick, day by day, disobedient act by disobedient act. The taller and stronger the wall becomes, the harder it is to hear God's voice.

Let's take a look at one particular sin—unforgiveness. The Bible is very clear about the subject of forgiveness. In Matthew 18:21-25, Peter asked Jesus "Lord, how many times shall I forgive my brother when he sins against me? Up to seven times?"

Jesus answered, "I tell you, not seven times, but seventy-seven times."

It is no wonder Peter's next words were, "Increase our faith."

Sometimes I think I like Peter's ideas better—seven strikes and you're out. But Jesus tells us to put no limit on forgiving others, just as God has put no limit on forgiving His children. He even gave His only Son as a sacrifice, as a payment, to pay the penalty for our sins.

God's forgiveness should stir such love in us that we would long to forgive others in return. In Luke 7:36-50, a prostitute came to Jesus while He dined with a Pharisee. She wept, washed His feet with her tears, dried them with her hair, and anointed them with perfume. She was overcome with Christ's love and forgiveness. When the Pharisees questioned her acts, Jesus reminded them, "He who has been forgiven little loves little." She had been forgiven much—and as a result, loved much. I don't know about you, but I have been forgiven much!

What exactly is forgiveness? To forgive means to no longer use the offense against the offender. It has nothing to do with whether or not the offender deserves forgiveness. Most do not. I do not deserve God's forgiveness, and yet He has forgiven me. Forgiving is taking someone off of your hook and placing him or her on God's hook. It is a gift you give yourself and more about what you do than what was done to you.

Amazingly, many times the person we are holding a grudge against isn't even aware of it or doesn't care about the ill feelings.

Ultimately, the only person being hurt is the person refusing to forgive. In essence, when we don't forgive, it is as though we are trying to punish the person by banging our own heads against the wall and saying, "Here, take that!" As I mentioned before, perhaps the person doesn't *deserve* to be forgiven. Perhaps you don't want to let the offender off the hook. None of us deserves to be forgiven, but look at how God forgave you and me. If we got what we deserved, we would all be sentenced to eternity in hell. But God gives us grace (receiving what we don't deserve) and mercy (not receiving what we do deserve).

A dramatic turning point in my own spiritual journey was when I realized that I had not forgiven my father for the mistakes he had made during my childhood. I had reached a plateau in my life and couldn't seem to move forward. I didn't know what to do about my future and could not detect God leading me one way or the other. During an extended time of prayer with a mentor, he asked me if I had forgiven my father for his past failures. I knew I had not. So that night I forgave my dad and God put an incredible love for him in the place where resentment had been.

This was a very dramatic turning point in my life—as a daughter and as a child of God. I am not saying that when you offer forgiveness, you'll strike it rich, find the man of your dreams, or live happily ever after. I'm not saying that you will instantaneously begin hearing God's voice at all times. However, I do believe that unforgiveness can block God's power in our lives, inhibit our ability to hear His voice, and cause us to miss out on a storehouse of blessings.

Here's a test to see how serious you are about hearing God's voice. Has God begun to convict you of a wall of sin that could be blocking your ability to hear His voice or feel His gentle nudges? Is there someone you need to forgive? Are you willing to obey right now? If not, I suggest you place a bookmark on this page, close the book, and come back to this same spot when you are ready to proceed.

There are many walls of sin we can build in our lives. Whatever wall of sin the Holy Spirit brings to our attention, He does so for one reason. Not to condemn us, but to bring us to repentance and set us free. There is good news here! Just as sin can keep you from listening to God, listening to God can keep you from sin.

Led Astray

One spring we decided to let our golden retriever, Ginger, get "married." Shortly thereafter, she gave birth to seven golden balls of fur—two males and five females. I called one of the adoptive parents just a few hours after delivery.

"Cynthia, this is Sharon. The puppies are here! We have the pick of the litter set aside for you—a fine fat butterball of a male. What shall we call him?"

"Fletcher!" her three children yelled in the background.

Seven weeks and many bags of Puppy Chow later, we delivered Fletcher to the Shangri-la of the dog world. Our friends, Larry and Cynthia Price, and their three children, live in a home surrounded by 30 acres of undeveloped forestland. As we drove down their mile-long driveway carved through 60-foot pine trees, I imagined Fletcher thinking of his siblings and musing, "If they could see me now!"

For the next seven years, Fletcher's days consisted of roaming through the forest, sniffing out snakes and raccoons, chasing deer and terrifying their young, and taking naps with possums or any other creatures that happened to wander into the Prices' backyard. On days that he got overheated from all his adventures, he practiced his dog paddling in the nearby pond. His only concern in life was Larry and the tweezers he used nightly to remove ticks that hitchhiked on their furry host.

One day, Cynthia got a call from a friend in the city. "Cynthia, this is Lynette. We're going out of town for a week, and I hate to put our dog in the kennel for that long. Would you mind if she came out to your place and spent the week while we're gone?"

"Sure, bring her on over. Fletcher will like the company." And boy, did he!

After being properly introduced and sniffing each other in a circular motion for a few minutes, the two new friends were off and running. Fletcher commenced to show Roxy the ropes of country living. "Here's how you chase a deer. Watch out for those hooves! These snakes are really fun to bark at. How about this pond mud! I bet you don't have anything like this in the city." The dogs were a furry blur of activity.

Two days later, Cynthia noticed the couple bounding down the mile-long driveway, only this time, Roxy was in the lead. A few hours later, the family realized that the two dogs were gone. For the first time in seven years, Fletcher had left the safety and security of his haven, led astray by his new friend.

Larry and the kids searched everywhere, but came up empty-handed. After a sleepless night, Cynthia had an idea. Even though the Boyds, Roxy's owners, had moved from their house in town nearly three years ago, she had an urge to drive by their old address.

"Fletcher! Roxy!" she called from her car window in front of her friends' former address.

Slowly but surely, two filthy mutts emerged from under the house with tails tucked and heads hanging low.

"You bad dogs," Cynthia chided. "Get in the car this instant!"

Cynthia drove the two renegades home and promptly chained Roxy to a tree. "Girl, your vacation is over."

The next day, Larry went outside to feed Fletcher and his way-ward friend, but Fletcher was gone. Again, they searched the streets, the highways, and even their friends' old address. But this time, there was no dog. This time, their pet was gone for good.

Before Roxy, Fletcher had lived a happy and contented life without a care in the world. His abode was the dog version of the Garden of Eden, surrounded by a loving family and with every possible desire right at his paw tips. But then a new buddy came along who wanted to show him there was more to life than the secure confines of the 30-acre woods. The enticing Roxy led her stable companion astray. Once he had tasted the forbidden fruit, once he had sniffed the foreign smells, the pull toward the tempting new land was too strong.

I know Fletcher is a dog and incapable of reason, but what a picture of temptation! First Corinthians 15:33 says, "Do not be misled: 'Bad company corrupts good character.'" The Amplified version of that same verse states it this way, "Do not be so deceived and misled! Evil companionships (communion, associations) corrupt and deprave good manners and morals and character." When we allow someone to lead us into an area where we should not go, to eat a fruit that we should not eat, to gaze at that which we should not look, or to seek sustenance from some source other than God, we are setting ourselves up as strays instead of members of a loving family. The temptation may appear exciting and adventurous at first, but the end leaves us scavenging for what was once freely given—love, nourishment, and protection.

Fletcher never returned. Never again did he hear his master's voice.

Temptation

Before I leave this section on tall walls of sin that block our reception and prevent us from hearing God's voice in our lives, I want to mention the difference between temptation and sin. The Bible says of Jesus, "For we do not have a high priest who is unable to sympathize with our weaknesses, but we have one who has been tempted in every way, just as we are—yet was without sin" (Hebrews 4:15). I think of it this way. When I turn on my computer in the morning and check my e-mail, sometimes I can receive some pretty disgusting invitations. "Click here for a hot time" or "Someone wants to meet you, click here." Those e-mails are not my fault. I don't even know how they got to my computer. They are not a sin on my part. However, when does going to their Web site or answering their e-mail become a sin? The moment I accept the invitation.

I believe that Satan sends us e-mails (evil-mails) all day long. We have a choice to accept or reject the invitation to sin. As I've often heard, "You can't prevent birds from flying over your head, but you can keep them from building a nest in your hair!" After Jesus had been in the desert praying and fasting for 40 days, Satan came and tempted Him in the same three areas of His life that he had tempted Eve. He tempted Him in His body (turn these stones to food), in His soul (You can have authority over all You see), and in His spirit (throw Yourself down from this cliff and watch the angels lift You up). Each time Satan hissed a temptation, Jesus fought back with the Sword of the Spirit—the Word of God. "It is written: 'Man does not live on bread alone'" (Luke 4:4). "It is written: 'Worship the Lord your God and serve him only'" (Luke 4:8). "It is written: 'Do not put the Lord your God to the test'" (Luke 4:12).

Jesus showed us how to fight temptation—with the Word of Truth. But we have to know the Word in order to be able to fight temptation with the Word.

If you hear a voice tempting you to sin, you can be sure it is not God's voice you are hearing. "When tempted, no one should say, 'God is tempting me.' For God cannot be tempted by evil, nor does he tempt anyone; but each one is tempted when, by his own evil desire, he is dragged away and enticed. Then, after desire has conceived, it gives birth to sin; and sin, when it is full-grown, gives birth to death" (James 1:13-15).

After Satan left Jesus, Luke records, "When the devil had finished all this tempting, he left him until an opportune time" (Luke 4:13). Oh my, he just never quits. But here's the praise, here's the promise, here's the providential provision: "No temptation has seized you except what is common to man. And God is faithful; he will not let you be tempted beyond what you can bear. But when you are tempted, he will also provide a way out so that you can stand up under it" (1 Corinthians 10:13). I don't know about you, but that gives me great hope—and great responsibility to take the way of escape.

Remember, if you are hearing a voice calling you to sin, it is not God's voice. If you are hearing a voice urging you to walk away from temptation, it is the Holy Spirit telling you not to lay one more brick on the wall of sin that blocks your reception to hearing God's voice.

Shoo, Fly

A little florescent green fly with transparent wings positioned itself on the dashboard of my car like a runner on his mark waiting for the shot to be fired. Then it torpedoed into the windshield at breakneck speed, only to bounce back as though it had been hit by an electrical current. Confused by this invisible barrier, it perched on the dashboard once again and strategized its next move while rubbing its tiny little hands together.

Suddenly, it shot forward with all its might, only to once again bounce off the force field and land panting on the dash. Then in one final act of desperation and frustration, it angrily attacked the glass at seven pops per second.

Feeling rather sorry for this insect, I rolled down my window and spoke softly to my captured friend. "Look, little fly, the window is open. Feel the wind? Here it is—your way of escape."

But the fly was knocked silly and lay recuperating on the dashboard, oblivious to the freedom just inches away. After a few seconds, I realized that it was not going to escape on its own volition, so I used my hand to shoo it in the direction of the open window. It resisted like a young puppy on a leash but finally made its way to the opening. However, instead of jumping at the chance of freedom, the little green fly with the bulging eyes just sat there with its wings pinned back by 60-mile-per-hour winds.

"Go on," I coaxed. "What are you afraid of?" I could not believe that I was talking to a fly and taking my eyes off the road to rescue a bug. Finally it became evident that Mr. Fly was not going to take this leap of faith, so I gave it that little extra push it needed, and off it flew.

Why was I so concerned for this silly fly? Pity, I guess. It was trying so hard to get free, and the way of escape was so close. This is a common problem for flies and humans alike. Whether it's King David being tempted to glance at Bathsheba taking a late-night bath on her rooftop or one of us being tempted to watch an unhealthy television program, there is always a way of escape. There is always an open window just a few steps away.

It's the same way with forgiveness or unforgiveness. God has told us that when we forgive, we set the offender free, but perhaps more importantly, we set ourselves free. When we have unforgiveness in our hearts, we are much like that little fly banging his head against the invisible force field. We try to fly. We try to soar. But something holds us back. We bang our heads on an invisible force field and lie dizzy and frustrated at our inability to move forward.

If we could hear the fly tell of its adventure of entrapment and escape, it might sound something like this. "I flew into a place where I thought I would find pleasure, but instead I found bondage. When I tried to get away, some invisible force kept me a prisoner. I banged my head against an unseen barrier time and time again. As I staggered to gain my composure and wait for the room to stop spinning, I saw an open window and a big hand coaxing me to come. My faltering steps led me to a ledge where I felt the wind on my face. I stood on the edge of freedom, unable to take that next step, when that gentle hand gave me the push I needed and out I flew. I was free."

A common tale of flies and men. Let's always look for the way of escape and experience the freedom that is ours when we listen to and obey our heavenly Father who loves us.

TWELVE

Spiritual Depletion

MRS. JAYNES, WAS YOUR BATTERY CHARGED?" This was the third question the cell phone operator asked as we were trying to figure out why I had such poor reception. If I'm not hearing God's voice through His Word, through the Holy Spirit's prompting, through prayer, other people, my circumstances, or nature, it may be that my spiritual battery is low on power.

Just before Jesus went to the cross, He told the disciples about a new power that would come and live within them once He had ascended to heaven. "But you will receive power when the Holy Spirit comes on you; and you will be my witnesses in Jerusalem, and in all Judea and Samaria, and to the ends of the earth" (Acts 1:8). After Jesus' resurrection and before His ascension, He told the disciples, "Do not leave Jerusalem, but wait for the gift my Father promised, which you have heard me speak about. For John baptized with water, but in a few days you will be baptized with the Holy Spirit" (Acts 1:4-5). Jesus told those boys to stay put until they were spiritually charged with power from on high. The Greek word for "power" is *dunamis,* which is where we get the word "dynamite." They had already seen how well they responded under pressure without the Holy Spirit. Most of the disciples fled and hid when Jesus was arrested and Peter denied he even knew Jesus—three times.

So they waited. The group of disciples and several women went back to Jerusalem, locked themselves in an upstairs room, and prayed. Then, on the Day of Pentecost, He came. The Holy Spirit came in the form of a rushing wind and what appeared to be tongues of fire that rested on their heads. Then Peter, filled with the Holy Spirit, stood and preached his most powerful sermon to date, and 3000 men and women accepted Jesus as the Christ. That's power! That's dynamite!

Jesus promised that the Holy Spirit would not be taken away from believers. However, we can live more or less under the Holy Spirit's influence at any given time. Paul wrote, "Do not get drunk on wine, which leads to debauchery. Instead, be filled with the Spirit" (Ephesians 5:18). The words "be filled" in the Greek are present tense and denote a continuous action. It could read *be filled and keep being filled.* "The Greek present tense is used to indicate that the filling of the Spirit is not a once-for-all experience. Repeatedly, as the occasion requires, the Spirit empowers for worship, service and testimony."[1] It is no accident that Paul compares and contrasts being filled with the Holy Spirit with being filled with wine. Just as a person can be under the influence of alcohol, she can be under the influence of the Spirit.

Even Jesus Christ Himself did not begin His public ministry until He received the power of the Holy Spirit (Matthew 3:13-17). "You know what has happened throughout Judea, beginning in Galilee after the baptism that John preached—how God anointed Jesus of Nazareth with the Holy Spirit and power, and how he went around doing good and healing all who were under the power of the devil, because God was with him" (Acts 10:37-38). Yes, Jesus was filled with the Holy Spirit, but that Spirit was released as He moved from place to place and ministered to people. When a woman who had been bleeding for twelve years touched Jesus' garment in order to be healed, "Jesus realized that power had gone out from him" (Mark 5:30).

So how do we continue to be filled with the Holy Spirit? Jesus shows us by example. "Very early in the morning, while it was still dark, Jesus got up, left the house and went off to a solitary place, where he prayed" (Mark 1:35). Our time in prayer and God's Word is the "filling station" where God fills us anew with His precious Holy Spirit. Someone once said, "Yes, we do receive the gift of the Holy Spirit at salvation, but I guess we must have a leak!" I'm not sure about the theology of that statement, but I do know that Scripture tells us to be filled and keep being filled.

Paul prayed this for the believers in various churches,

> I pray also that the eyes of your heart may be enlightened in order that you may know the hope to which he has called you, the riches of his glorious inheritance in the saints, and his incomparably *great power* for us who believe. That *power* is like the working of his mighty strength, which he exerted in Christ when he raised him from the dead and seated him at his right hand in the heavenly realms, far above all rule and authority, power and dominion, and every title that can be given, not only in the present age but also in the one to come. And God placed all things under his feet and appointed him to be head over everything for the church, which is his body, the fullness of him who fills everything in every way (Ephesians 1:18-23, emphasis added).

Again Paul said,

> I pray that out of his glorious riches he may strengthen you with *power* through his Spirit in your inner being, so that Christ may dwell in your hearts through faith. And I pray that you, being rooted and established in love, may have *power,* together with all the saints, to grasp how wide and long and high and deep is the love of Christ, and to know this love that

surpasses knowledge—that you may be filled to the measure of all the fullness of God. Now to him who is able to do immeasurably more than all we ask or imagine, according to his *power* that is at work within us, to him be glory in the church and in Christ Jesus throughout all generations, for ever and ever! Amen (Ephesians 3:16-21, emphasis added).

God warns us that we can become hard of hearing by resisting, quenching, or grieving the Holy Spirit. I never really understood what grieving the Holy Spirit meant until I had a child of my own. When Steven disobeyed or did not heed my warnings or teachings, it was much more than rule-breaking. It was heartbreaking. So it is when we disobey or ignore the Holy Spirit. As with a parent who watches her disobedient child, it breaks His heart.

A woman who listens to God is one who prays each day, "Lord, fill me afresh with Your Holy Spirit. Like an empty cup, I am ready to receive. May Your power fill every nook and cranny of my being and spill over to those with whom I come in contact this day. Amen."

Living Off the Saw Box

I couldn't stand it another day. For almost a year, my family had been crammed into a tiny rental house while our new home was being constructed. Boxes were stacked to the ceiling. Our bedroom furniture was wall-to-wall in a room with just enough space for a path that led to the bathroom. The 1950 Frigidaire needed constant defrosting, and the orange-and-yellow flowered wallpaper wasn't starting to grow on me. The kitchen was so tiny I could cook, clean, and serve the meal while standing in one spot and rotating my body 360 degrees. The one positive aspect of this cramped lifestyle was I could vacuum the entire house in ten minutes and only move the plug once!

The six-month building project was nearing its eleventh month and I wanted out!

"Clyde," I told the builder, "ready or not, I'm movin' in."

"Mrs. Jaynes, your house is on a hill and you don't have a driveway. How are you going to get your stuff up that muddy mountain?" the builder asked.

"I don't know, but if Moses can move one million people across the desert without a freeway, I can get our belongings up that hill without a driveway."

"But Mrs. Jaynes, the walls aren't even painted yet and the sheet rock's exposed."

"That's okay. We'll paint it later," I replied.

"But all the appliances aren't even installed," he argued.

"That's fine. I like takeout," I answered.

"But, Mrs. Jaynes, there's no electricity!"

Now I have to admit, he had me stumped on this one. Then I noticed an electric power saw sitting on a pile of 2 x 4s with a cord that plugged into a box on the telephone pole.

"Wait a minute. If there's no electricity, how can you use electric power saws to cut this lumber?" I asked.

"Well," he replied, "that little box on the telephone pole is called a saw box. The power company installs them on construction sites, and they provide just enough electricity to juice up the construction equipment. It's not enough to run a house."

"Is it enough to turn my lights on?" I asked.

"Some of them. But not too many at one time," he answered.

Seeing where I was going with this line of reasoning, the builder knew what I was thinking.

"Okay, Mrs. Jaynes, here's the deal. Yes, you can live in this house with power coming only from the saw box. You can turn on a few lights, but not all of them. If you want to take a hot shower, you've got to turn off everything else in the house and turn on the hot water heater for about 30 minutes. After you shower, you have to flip the water heater back off and flip the lights back on. You can turn on the oven, but you can't have anything else on at the same time. You don't have that much power available. If you move into this house, it will be like camping out in a very nice tent."

Yea! I had won! We climbed up the muddy mountain with all our belongings, moved into our new house, and lived off power from the saw box. At first it was an exciting adventure. Then after two weeks it was a lot of trouble. I grew impatient waiting 30 minutes for the water to heat up and instead settled for quick cold showers. I became tired of take-out food, and eating by candlelight no longer created a romantic mood. The little rental house was looking better all the time, and I, like the Israelites who were freed from captivity but wandered in the desert, longed for the good ol' days.

This all took place in November, and the chilly autumn air made for crisp mornings in a house with no heat. While reading my Bible by the warmth and rays of the early morning sunlight coming through the kitchen window, I came across the following verse: "You shall receive *power* when the Holy Spirit has come upon you" (Acts 1:8 NASB, emphasis added). "Ah," I whispered, "There's that word *power* again. I could use some of that about now." I flipped over a few pages and read Peter's first sermon after he had received the power of the Holy Spirit. I thought to myself, "Now that was dynamite!"

My mind flipped through the verses stored in my mind, and I thought of Ephesians 1:13, which promised the Holy Spirit to all who believe, and to Jesus' promise to the disciples in John 14:13. I closed my Bible and looked up at the saw box nailed to the telephone pole. Then God reminded me that He has given me the same power He had given Peter, but instead of living as though I have power of dynamite, I tend to walk around like a sparkler. Instead of walking in full power, I tend to settle for the limited power of the saw box.

Well, eventually, the electric company hooked us up to the main power source and we flipped on all the circuit breakers at one time. I made a commitment to never live off a saw box again. And in my spiritual life, I never want to settle for just enough of the Holy Spirit's power to barely function. I want it all. I want *dunamis* power, all circuits open, full throttle, full steam ahead. When I mentioned this to God, He reminded me that the power has always been available; I just need to choose to connect to the main power source and be recharged every day.

THIRTEEN

Retracted Antennas

I KNOW THIS IS THE NEW MILLENNIUM, but I still get a little embarrassed shopping in the lingerie department. Yes, I realize everybody wears underwear, but something about mulling around racks of panties makes me uncomfortable.

One day I was shopping for unmentionables when I noticed an elderly gentleman who looked even more uncomfortable than I did. Apparently, this man's wife was shopping for her new bloomers, and he was trying his best to casually avoid the area altogether. The lingerie department was across the aisle from the children's clothing department. This elderly gentleman strolled up and down in this buffer zone, taking an intense interest in the latest fall fashions for girls sizes 2–6x. His head stayed sharply turned to the right to avoid peeping at the ladies' personals on the left.

Mr. Man did a good job of not looking at the ladies' undies but a bad job of looking where his steps were going. What he did not see was that he was on a collision course with a lady mannequin, scantily almost dressed in a transparent nightie. As he innocently meandered along with nightgowns on his left and girls' plaid jumpers on his right, Mr. Man ran smack-dab into Ms. Mannequin, knocking her off of her stand. He spun around at breakneck speed, and with the agility of Superman, caught Ms. Mannequin, nightie and all (or less), in his able arms just before she hit the floor. Before he could be caught red-handed (and red-faced), he placed Ms. Mannequin back on her stand, and as any gallant Southern gentleman would do, straightened up the see-through pj's she was almost wearing.

Satisfied that the lady was safe and secure, he resumed his stroll down the aisle. Only this time I noticed a little more spunk in his step and an extra inch added to his stature. He had run smack into what he had feared the most and came out victorious. He had also held a beautiful lady in his arms, if only for a moment, and helped her get back on her own two feet. What man wouldn't feel proud?

Like the elderly gentleman avoiding looking at the ladies' lingerie, there are many things in my life I try to avoid. Instead of *turning aside* to listen to God, I'll turn my head so far in the opposite direction I get a spiritual crick in my neck. As a matter of fact, many times when I've tried to ignore a problem or God's voice nudging me to address it, I end up running smack-dab into it. And then, like Mr. Man, I am forced to look the problem squarely in the face. It would be much easier to listen to God while I'm still standing on my feet than to wait until I'm sprawled out on the floor with disaster lying in my arms.

Have you been avoiding God's voice? Have you placed your hands over your ears or eyes? Are you afraid of what He's going to say? I think sometimes we tend to lower our spiritual antennas out of fear. Proverbs 3:5-6 says, "Trust in the Lord with all your heart and lean not on your own understanding; in all your ways acknowledge him, and he will make your paths straight."

Do you remember the third question my friend the cell phone operator asked regarding possibilities for my poor reception? Was my antenna up? Just like the man who didn't want to see where he was going, I believe sometimes we retract our spiritual antennas because we don't really want to hear God's voice. This was the case with the children of Israel after Moses had led them out of Egypt. They decided they no longer wanted God to speak directly to them, but to speak only through Moses. Let's join them at Mount Sinai and listen to what occurred.

> On the morning of the third day there was thunder and lightning, with a thick cloud over the mountain, and a very loud trumpet blast. Everyone in the camp trembled. Then Moses led the people out of the camp to meet with God, and they stood at the foot of the mountain. Mount Sinai was covered with smoke because the LORD descended on it in fire. The smoke billowed up from it like smoke, from a furnace, the whole mountain trembled violently, and the sound of the trumpet grew louder and louder. Then Moses spoke and the voice of God answered him (Exodus 19:16-19).

As the Israelites gathered around the base of the mountain, God spoke audibly and proclaimed the Ten Commandments, which He had written with His hand on two tablets of stone. After that experience, the Israelites told Moses, "Speak to us yourself and we will listen. But do not have God speak to us or we will die" (Exodus 20:19).

They grew afraid of God and put their spiritual antennas down.

How many times have we been like those Israelites who didn't want to hear God's voice? We listen to a pastor but don't expect God to speak to us. We take notes from a respected Bible teacher but don't take the time to search the Scriptures for ourselves. We tune into a radio personality rather than tune into our heavenly Father, who longs to speak words of encouragement, instruction, and truth.

I think sometimes we are afraid of what He's going to tell us, and yet He has already promised us blessings if we obey. "For I know the plans I have for you," declares the LORD, "plans to prosper you and not to harm you, plans to give you hope and a future" (Jeremiah 29:11).

Also, I believe there are times we put our spiritual antennas down because we know what God would say to a certain situation and we don't want to hear it. Herod didn't want to listen to John the Baptist tell him it was wrong for him to be living with his sister-in-law. Not only did he put his spiritual antenna down, he beheaded the messenger. Time and time again, people in the Old Testament ignored God's voice speaking through the prophets. "For I called but you did not answer, I spoke but you did not listen" (Isaiah 65:12; see also 66:4). After a while, God grew tired of talking to those who would not listen, and He placed His hand over His mouth. Between the last book of the Old Testament and the first book of the New, there was a famine of God's voice more than 400 years. "'The days are coming,'" declares the Sovereign LORD, "'when I will send a famine through the land—not a famine of food or a thirst for water, but a famine of hearing the words of the LORD'" (Amos 8:11). I cannot think of any worse plight than a famine of God's words.

How do we keep our spiritual ears "tuned in" to God's voice? As I mentioned earlier, "walk in the Spirit." When we walk in the Spirit, we have our spiritual antennas raised and ready to receive.

Why do we "tune God out"? Could it be that we don't want to hear what He's telling us because we want to be in control? We don't want anyone telling us what to do? That was part of Eve's problem in the Garden of Eden, and I don't think we've changed much over the past several thousand years. The rich young ruler stopped listening because he didn't want to give up his money and lose control. The Pharisees stopped listening because they didn't want to give up their prestigious temple positions and lose control. Pharaoh stopped listening to Moses because he didn't want to free the Egyptian slaves and lose control.

I have some deaf friends, and it always amuses me when they get in an argument with each other or with their hearing compatriots. If they don't want to "listen," they simply turn their heads where they can't see the other person's signs. Boy, is that frustrating! It gives new meaning to turning a deaf ear.

To become women who listen to God, we need to raise our antennas high and approach God with open eyes to see and open ears to hear.

Mrs. Jaynes, You're Leading Again

My husband and I had been married about ten years when we read *His Needs, Her Needs* by Willard Harley. In the book, Mr. Harley suggested that couples spend about 15 hours a week giving each other their undivided attention communicating or sharing some recreational activity. Steve and I were well off the mark of 15 hours, so we decided to take Harley's advice and find some activity that we would both enjoy doing together. Steve suggested golf and I suggested ballroom dancing. After one look at my golf swing, we headed straight to the ballroom dance studio and signed up for a six-week introductory course.

Steve and I had traveled many times to a resort in Sea Island, Georgia, and watched couples as they glided around the dance floor, moving as one to the fluid sounds of a professional orchestra playing music from the Big Band era. That's what I wanted to do. I wanted us to be the next Ginger Rogers and Fred Astaire.

"Dr. and Mrs. Jaynes," the instructor began, "the first thing we will learn is the fox-trot. Dr. Jaynes, you place your right hand on your wife's left shoulder blade. Cup it firmly in your hand." Then she turned to me, "Mrs. Jaynes, you gently rest your left hand on your husband's right shoulder."

So far, so good, we all agreed.

She then proceeded to teach us to make little boxes with our feet while counting 1-2-3-4, 1-2-3-4, slow-slow-quick-quick, slow-slow-quick-quick. This was not floating across the floor. I felt more like a shopping buggy being pushed around the perimeter of the mirrored room.

The instructor continued. "Dr. Jaynes, you have the hardest part because it is up to you to lead. All the woman has to do is follow."

More than once, she tapped me on the shoulder and said, "Mrs. Jaynes, you're leading again." The problem was, when I led, Steve wouldn't follow. I know a train can't have two engines, but I felt I was the better dancer and the lessons would go much quicker if Steve would just let me lead. (Goodness, isn't that what Eve said in the Garden?)

I quickly became bored with the little boxes and asked, "Can't we learn to move around the room a little instead of standing in one place?"

So we moved on to phase two—"gliding" around the room. Instead of making small boxes with our feet, we learned to make small boxes with a flap open. We took two steps sideways and two steps forward. Actually, Steve got to move forward, but I had to move backward, which seemed totally unfair to me. Now, I understand that we couldn't both move forward, but why was I the one who had to move backward? The instructor rolled her eyes and assured me that this was the way God planned it. (She didn't explain it exactly that way, but I knew that's what she meant.)

I had wanted to be Ginger Rogers, and yet I looked more like Fred Rogers than Ginger. All the while, the instructor kept tapping me on the shoulder and saying, "Mrs. Jaynes, you're leading again."

Another lesson we had to learn was to not look down at our feet but at each other's face. "Concentrate on looking in each other's eyes," the instructor said. "Looking at your feet will not make them do the right steps. You just need to listen to the music and let your feet move you around the room."

Yeah, right, I thought. I felt better looking down, as if my eyes could will my feet into moving correctly. Eventually, I did learn to keep my eyes off of my feet and on my leader's handsome face.

After our first 45-minute class was complete, the instructor warned, "Now you must go home and practice. If you don't practice what you've learned, you'll forget everything we've gone over today." Let's just say she was right.

Hebrews 5:14 states, "Solid food is for the mature, who *because of practice* have their senses trained to discern good and evil" (NASB, emphasis added). It takes practice to tune our ears to hearing God's voice, and it takes practice to follow His lead. Just as I had to learn to let my husband lead on the dance floor, I've had to learn to let God lead in the dance of life.

The truth is, the Leader does have the hardest part. And guess what—He knows all the steps! All we need to do is gently place our hand on His strong shoulder, avoid looking at our own feet, and keep our eyes focused on Him.

FOURTEEN

Unbelief

It was a terrifying three weeks for those living in the Washington, D.C., area. One man was shot in the chest while exiting a home improvement store, another while pumping gas, and a woman while she was loading her groceries into her car. All in all, ten people had lost their lives to the gunman and three had been wounded. Where were the bullets coming from? Who would take the lives of unsuspecting civilians as if they were clay disks at a shooting range? The police had tried for weeks to find the sniper or snipers, but to no avail. After each incident, the sniper disappeared into thin air like a villain in a superhero fantasy.

Trucker Ron Lantz from Ludlow, Kentucky, was five runs away from retirement. He had enjoyed his life on the open highways and byways, but in just a few days he would turn the key for the last time and head for home. One thing he was going to miss about parking his rig was his trucking buddies who gathered to pray. On October, 17, 2002, as they zigzagged across the country, dozens of truckers, including Ron, radioed each other agreeing to gather at a remote rest stop to pray that the sniper would soon be caught. "We prayed for the families of those killed by the sniper," Ron later told friend Larry Dillon. "We prayed that someone would stop him. We knew the prayer was going to be answered. One time or another. That's the way we believe."[1]

A few days later, just 20 miles away from where the group had gathered to pray, Ron was listening to the radio. As he was driving again through the D.C. area, he felt compelled to pull off the highway at a rest stop. When he did, he spotted a car fitting the description of the one police had described as the would-be assassin's—a blue Chevrolet Caprice. Carefully trying to read the license plate, a chill ran down his spine as he realized the numbers matched. He quickly called 911 and then waited for what seemed like the longest 15 minutes of his life until the police arrived. He pulled his truck across one of the exits in an effort to block the murderer's escape.

The police arrived in full force, pulled not one, but two snipers from the car, along with guns, ammunition, and a tripod. The nightmare was over.

"I just want people to think what I did is what I should have done. I am no hero at this, no hero whatsoever. I don't even want to be thought of as a hero."

When I read about Ron Lantz, my immediate thought was, *he is a hero!* Not because he found the snipers, but because he was a man who listened to God. Ron prayed with great faith and believed God would answer. When he felt the Holy Spirit's nudge, he obeyed and acted. That sounds like the definition of a hero to me. Whether it's Moses in the Old Testament or the apostle Paul in the New, whether it's Ron Lantz or me or you, a person who knows how to listen to God's voice and has the courage to obey is a hero. "Blessed is the man [or woman] who listens to me, watching daily at my doors, waiting at my doorway" (Proverbs 8:34).

Now let's look at the final problem with my cell phone reception. Why was I able to send a call but unable to receive a call? This made no sense to me. When I asked the operator about this twist, she replied, "It takes more cell strength to receive a call than to send a call."

This response had me pondering my prayer life for quite some time. It doesn't take more *power* per se to listen to God than to talk to God, but I think it does take more faith—and faith is where the power lies.

One of the major reasons Christians don't hear God's voice today is because they don't believe He still speaks, or at least they don't believe He would speak to them. Even in the New Testament, Jesus' disciples were surprised when God answered their prayers. In the book of Acts, when Peter was arrested and thrown into prison, a group of believers gathered to pray for his release. But when God answered their prayer and Peter stood knocking at their door, they didn't believe it was him. A servant girl named Rhoda came to answer the door, and when she recognized Peter's voice, she ran back and told the others, forgetting to let their answer to prayer in.

"You're out of your mind," they told her. But after she kept insisting it was him, they opened the door and welcomed Peter back home (Acts 12:12-16).

I do that from time to time. I pray for a certain situation, but then I'm surprised when God answers, or I even miss His answer altogether. Why? I think because deep down I don't expect Him to speak.

David was a man who expected God to speak to him on a daily basis. He wrote, "In the morning, O LORD, you hear my voice; in the morning I lay my requests before you and wait in expectation" (Psalm 5:3).

In Luke chapter 2, we see a wonderful example of two people who had waited their entire lives for God to reveal the Messiah. God told Simeon that he would not die until he saw the One who would be called the Lord's Christ. Anna was an 84-year-old prophetess who had spent most of her life in the temple praying, fasting, and worshiping. When Mary and Joseph brought the baby Jesus to the temple to perform the purification ceremony required by Jewish Law, both of these elderly saints had their lifelong dream of seeing the Messiah fulfilled. God spoke to them and revealed this Hebrew child's true identity. While Jesus may have looked like hundreds of other Hebrew babies who had been presented in the temple, God spoke to Anna and Simeon—"This is the One you've been waiting for."

Why didn't the Pharisees and priests recognize Jesus? These were, after all, leaders who knew the Old Testament prophesies better than anyone. Could it be that their head knowledge did not translate into faith or heart knowledge? Could it be that they did not really expect God to show up? Could it be that God reveals Himself to those who are expecting Him?

Let's face it. We'd all like to hear God speak from a burning bush the way Moses did or from a bright light the way Saul did, but for most of us, hearing God's voice will rely on faith.

What is faith? "Now faith is the assurance (the confirmation, the title deed) of the things [we] hope for, being the proof of things [we] do not see and the conviction of their reality [faith perceiving as real fact what is not revealed to the senses]" (Hebrews 11:1 AMP). It is a gift we receive (Ephesians 2:8; 2 Peter 1:1), and each person is given a certain measure (Romans 12:3). But like a muscle, faith continues to grow stronger the more we use it.

When the disciples failed to cast out a demon and asked Jesus the reason, He answered, "Because you have so little faith" (Matthew 17:20). It was not the quantity of their faith but the quality. They didn't need more faith; they needed a stronger faith. Jesus went on to say, "I tell you the truth, if you have faith as small as a mustard seed, you can say to this mountain, 'Move from here to there' and it will move. Nothing will be impossible for you" (17:20). As we exercise the faith God has given to us, it will become stronger and stronger.

Let's look at Matthew 21:21-22 once again: "I tell you the truth, if you have faith and do not doubt, not only can you do what was done to the fig tree, but also you can say to this mountain, 'Go, throw yourself into the sea,' and it will be done. If you believe, you will receive whatever you ask for in prayer." Jesus used a shriveled fig tree to teach the disciples a lesson on faith and believing prayer. "But belief in the New Testament is never reduced to forcing oneself to 'believe' what one does not really believe. Instead, it is related to genuine trust in God and obedience to and discernment of his will."[2] You can't "muster up" faith. "Faith comes from hearing, and hearing by the Word of Christ" (Romans 10:17 NASB). The more we know God and His character, the stronger our faith in Him will become.

Does it take more power to hear from God than to talk to God? No, but I believe it does take more faith. Believe that God will answer your prayers. Believe that He will speak to you in your everyday life. Believe that you are the child of a Father who loves to talk to His children.

"Call to Me, and I will answer you, and I will tell you great and mighty things, which you do not know" (Jeremiah 33:3 NASB).

A Dirty Story

Jesus instructed His disciples to build their houses on the rock (Matthew 7:25). Of course, He was talking about building our spiritual houses on the solid foundation of Jesus Christ—The Rock. But when Steve and I built our home, we took that verse to heart and built our house on the rockiest soil in all of Mecklenburg County. After we moved in, the landscaper planted a nice stand of rye grass, but because of the poor quality of the soil, all the grass died within six months of sprouting. It was not a lawn you'd want to walk on with bare feet. Hiking boots were more like it. While I wanted to spend money on new curtains for the living room, a new sofa for the den, and a few pictures for the bare walls, Steve informed me that we were first going to have to invest hundreds of dollars for truckloads of dirt to cover our rocky soil.

Something about paying money for dirt did not sit well with me. I prayed for God to show us another solution.

A few days later I was driving down my street and noticed heavy tractors, backhoes, and dump trucks. A crew of men were digging a six-foot-deep trench to install a pipeline for the families at the front of the neighborhood who didn't have city water. I slowed down and there before me was a beautiful sight. Piles and piles of dirt! One of the flagmen stopped me as a dump truck blocked the road. While my car was idling, my mind was in full gear. I felt as though God was saying, "Okay, girl, tell Me what you see."

"I see a big bulldozer. A dump truck. A big bulldozer emptying dirt in a big dump truck. A big potbellied man holding a stop sign with his tummy peeking through his shirt and his buttons about to pop open. I see a big potbellied man who probably likes to eat."

Then I had an idea. What do I need? Dirt. What does he have? Dirt. What would he like to have? Food. (I'm sure this was an inspired train of thought!)

I rolled down my window and waved at the flag-holding gentleman to come over to the car. Then I asked in my sweetest Southern drawl, "Excuse me, sir. What are you plannin' to do with all that little ol' dirt?"

"Well, I guess we'll haul it off som'wares," he replied.

"I'll tell you what," I bargained. "If you dump that ol' dirt in my yard over there, I'll make you and your men a German chocolate pie every day while you're here."

I could almost see his buttons getting tighter with visions of chocolate pies floating in his head. So for several weeks, I took German chocolate pies and six forks to the men working on the water pipes and they brought me truckloads of chocolate-colored dirt. By the end of the summer our yard looked like a mini mountain range with piles and piles of glorious dirt surrounding my house. In the fall, we hired someone with a tractor to spread out the mounds and we now have a luscious stand of grass.

Proverbs 31:16 says that the wife of noble character considers a field and buys it, and with her earning she plants a vineyard. I guess this was my version of buying a field. I just did it one truckload at a time. Instead of planting a vineyard, I purchased new curtains for the living room, a new sofa for the den, and a few pictures for the bare walls.

It's a dirty story—but with a sweet ending. As Henry Blackaby says in *Experiencing God,* "When you pray, look to see what happens next." You never know how God's going to answer a prayer.

PART IV

Bridges to Hearing
God's Voice

CLEARING OUR PLATES

❧

Today, more than ever before, our lives are filled with all sorts of stuff—just stuff. We have more boats, planes, cars, TVs, RVs, and CDs. We live in bigger houses, take more exotic vacations, eat at fancier restaurants, wear more expensive clothes, spend more time at salons, and work fewer hours. We have more books to keep us informed, more clothes to keep us fashionable, more entertainment to keep us relaxed, and more electronic gadgets to keep us efficient. With all this bigger and better and more, more, more, why aren't we more fulfilled? Our all-you-can-live buffet approach to life has not brought a sense of contentment or satisfaction to the society as a whole. Lives are filled but not fulfilled.

I'm not a fan of food bars or all-you-can-eat buffets. When you first approach a food bar, everything looks good, so you put a little of this and then a little of that on your plate. Before you know it, your plate is a mountain range of food and everything begins to taste the same. After such a meal, I never feel satisfied. Oh yes, I feel full, but not fulfilled. I feel stuffed, but not nourished.

We have the same experience when we approach the buffet, all-you-can-live lifestyle. We cram in more and more but feel less and less satisfied. A woman's life is a busy life. In the smorgasbord of activities and choices, we pile on cooking, grocery shopping, bill paying, repairmen calling, career juggling, doctor visits, dentist visits, ophthalmologist visits, carpools, church activities, exercise class, and baseball, soccer, basketball, football, dance, and gymnastic practices, just to name a few. Then there are the social clubs and the community needs. Our lives flip back and forth from one activity to another like those switchboard operators in the old black-and-white movies.

I believe it is only when we begin to clear our plates of the pabulum and make time to hear from God that we will experience true nourishment, satisfaction, and fulfillment. Let's take a look at how we prepare to listen to God and receive the blessings that are sure to follow.

FIFTEEN

Preparing to Listen to God

ANNE MORROW LINDBERGH ONCE TOOK a vacation on the East Coast for two weeks alone and wrote her reflective book, *Gift from the Sea*. In it she said,

> I began to understand why the saints were rarely married women. I am convinced it had nothing inherently to do, as I once supposed, with chastity or children. It has to do primarily with distractions. The bearing, rearing, feeding and educating of children; the running of a house with its thousand details; human relationships with their myriad pulls, women's normal occupations in general run counter to creative life, or contemplative life, or saintly life. The problem is not merely one of *Woman and Career, Woman and the Home, Woman and Independence*. It is more basically: how to remain whole in the midst of the distractions of life; how to remain balanced, no matter what centrifugal forces tend to

pull one off center; how to remain strong, no matter what shocks come in at the periphery and tend to crack the hub of the wheel. What is the answer? There is no easy answer, no complete answer. I have only clues, shells from the sea. The bare beauty of the channeled whelk tells me that one answer, and perhaps a first step, is in simplification of life, in cutting out some of the distractions. But how? Total retirement is not possible. I cannot shed my responsibilities. I cannot permanently inhabit a desert island. I cannot be a nun in the midst of family life. I would not want to be. The solution for me, surely, is neither in total renunciation of the world, nor in total acceptance of it. I must find a balance somewhere, or an alternative rhythm between these two extremes; a swinging of the pendulum between solitude and communion, between retreat and return.[1]

Thinking of Anne's pendulum, that pendulum of retreat and return swings (on a small scale) every morning as I begin my day with God. Then again, there are much larger swings when I retreat for a few days away in solitude, or in the other direction, must immerse myself in work to meet a deadline or family activities around various events. The danger comes when the pendulum becomes lodged between activities and unable or unwilling to swing back toward the retreat position.

Charles Spurgeon, a famous London pastor, once said that he was so tired and weary, he felt like a waiter at a wedding feast at which he longed to be the guest.[2] In my own life, I've had that same longing—to put down the mop and be a guest, to sit at Jesus' feet and get out of the kitchen. And when I think about it, that's the very invitation He gave the busy Martha of Bethany.

Nestled between the story of the Good Samaritan (Luke 10:30-37) and Jesus teaching the disciples how to pray (Luke 11:1-4) lies the familiar story of Mary and Martha. The Good Samaritan shows us how to work and The Lord's Prayer shows us how to worship. One deals with our relationship with men and the other with our relationship with God. The story of Mary and Martha is sandwiched in between and shows us how to balance them both. Martha was busy in the kitchen while Mary sat at Jesus' feet. When Martha complained, Jesus said, "Martha, Martha, you are worried and upset about many things, but only one thing is needed. Mary has chosen what is better, and it will not be taken away from her" (Luke 10:41-42). Jesus wasn't saying to abandon the kitchen. He was saying that we need to know when to work and when to worship.

Prioritizing Our Life

So how do we prepare ourselves for becoming women who listen to God's voice? It all begins with prioritizing our life and putting our relationship with Christ at the top of our list. In our book *A Woman's Secret to a Balanced Life* that I coauthored with Lysa TerKeurst, we paint a picture of seven key areas of a woman's life using the illustration of a series of seven waterfalls in Maui, Hawaii. At the end of the road to Hana, at the top of a mountain, rests a tranquil pool of water. When that pool is full, the water spills over by a spectacular waterfall to a second pool below. When the second pool is full, the water spills over to a third pool. The pools continue this process of filling and spilling until the water flowing from them forms a stair step of seven waterfalls and eventually spills out into the Pacific Ocean. These cascades are a portrait of a woman's life. The first pool is our relationship with Jesus Christ. Only when this pool is filled can we effectively flow in the other areas of our lives: marriage, motherhood, home, finances and time, friendships, and community.

The same is true when we talk about being a woman who listens to God. First and foremost, we must be continually filled with the Holy Spirit for the lines of communication to flow freely.

In his book *First Things First,* Stephen Covey tells the story of a man teaching a time management class. In order to make a point, the man pulled a wide-mouthed gallon jar from behind his podium. He then began placing fist-sized rocks into the jar until they reached the top. "Is the jar full?" he asked.

Some of the students, not knowing where he was going, blurted out, "Yes." The teacher laughed gently and said, "No, it's not." He pulled out a bucket of gravel and began to pour it in the jar. The class watched as the gravel filtered down between the rocks, filling the spaces until they reached the top.

"Is the jar full?"

A bit hesitant, the class remained silent. He then poured a bucket of sand down among the rocks and the pebbles. Once again, the small grains of sand filled in around the nooks and crannies until they reached the top of the jar. "Is the jar full?" And his students said, "Probably not."

Next the teacher reached for a pitcher and slowly poured water in the jar. It filtered down until it was running over the lip of the jar. "Now is the jar full?" the time management consultant asked. The class answered, "We think it is."

"The lesson is, class," he said, "if you don't put the big rocks in first, you'll never get them in later."[3]

This lesson had such an impact on my life that I now have two jars in my workroom. One is full of large fist-sized rocks and the other is three-fourths full of sand. The two jars serve as a reminder to begin my day with the big rocks in my life (my time alone with God), and all the errands and to-do lists (which are as endless as grains of sand) will fall nicely into place.

Scheduling Daily Retreats

Have you ever wondered how Jesus knew what He was to do each day as the sun rose over the horizon? Some of His greatest moments were followed by extensive times of prayer. He spent all night in prayer before He chose His disciples (Luke 6:12). He defeated Satan's temptations after praying and fasting for 40 days (Matthew 4:3-11). Prayer preceded His miracles (John 11:42-43) and gave Him the strength to go to the cross (Luke 22:39-42).

In Mark 1:35 (NASB), we see Jesus' pattern for prayer. "And in the early morning, while it was still dark, He arose and went out and departed to a lonely place, and was praying there." If Jesus Christ, God's Son, needed to spend time alone with His heavenly Father before the start of each new day, then how much more do I?

Notice that when the disciples looked for Jesus, they always knew where to find Him—praying. Mark 1:36-38 goes on to say that while Jesus was praying, Simon and his companions searched for Him, found Him, and said to Him, "Everyone is looking for You" (verse 37). The disciples saw that the people in the town where Jesus had been the day before wanted Him to return. However, Jesus replied, "Let us go somewhere else—to the nearby villages—so I can preach there also. That is why I have come" (verse 38). Jesus had received His "marching orders" from God and He was not going to let the tyranny of the urgent divert His purpose.

I don't know about you, but by 8:30 in the morning my phone is ringing with all kinds of requests and demands that threaten to pull me in several directions. By spending time in prayer with God first thing in the morning, my spirit becomes more tuned in to the Holy Spirit, and I am able to hear His voice more clearly throughout the day. Thus, I am able to say yes and no more confidently as various opportunities arise.

Let's take a look at the daily retreat. The best way for me to become a woman who listens to God on a daily basis is to begin each day tuning in to His presence. For me, this includes reading my Bible, meditating on Scripture, and praying. I pray before I read, as I read, and then after I read. My prayer during the time I'm reading the Bible is more of a dialogue. "Lord, as I read today, open my eyes to see what You would have me see. Open my heart to receive a fresh word from You. Open my ears to hear what You would have me hear."

Then I pick a particular passage. Sometimes I read through a book of the Bible over a given amount of time, and other times I choose a passage I feel He's leading me to. Sometimes the Holy Spirit will draw me to a particular verse or even a particular word.

For example, as I was reading the book of John, I noticed that he used the word "truth" time and time again. So I went back and meditated on every verse that had the word "truth" in it and asked God to show me what He wanted me to understand about "truth."

Another time I focused on the words "in Christ," found in the book of Ephesians approximately 40 times. I prayed that God would show me what it meant to be "in Christ." Amazingly, He's still showing me what that means today.

When I come across a certain Scripture that I feel is God's particular or *rhema* word for me, I pray about that verse and ask God to show me how to apply it to my life. "Lord, help me to guard my words as You said in Psalm 141:3," or "Lord, show me someone who needs encouragement today as I read in 1 Thessalonians 5:11." My time of prayer that follows Bible reading is more intense. During this time I generally begin by praising God for who He is and thanking Him for what He's done. I pray for the needs of others and for myself, and then I end the time thanking God again.

As I mentioned before, hearing God's voice through the Scriptures requires meditation. This is more than reading the Bible for information. "You will seek me and find me when you seek me with all your heart" (Jeremiah 29:13). When we meditate on God's Word, it is an invitation for Him to open our heart, mind, and soul to understand and receive what He wants us to receive.

Author J.I. Packer gives this definition of meditation:

> Meditation is the activity of calling to mind, and thinking over, and dwelling on, and applying to oneself, the various things that one knows about the works and ways and purposes and promises of God. It is an activity of holy thought, consciously performed in the presence of God, under the eye of God, by the help of God as a means of communion with God. Its purpose is to clear one's mental and spiritual vision of God, and to let His truth make its full and proper impact on one's mind and heart. It is

a matter of talking to oneself about God and oneself; it is, indeed, often a matter of arguing with oneself, reasoning oneself out of moods of doubt and unbelief into a clear apprehension of God's power and grace. Its effect is to ever humble us as we contemplate God's greatness and glory, and our own littleness and sinfulness and to encourage and reassure us—"comfort" us in the old, strong Bible sense of the word—as we contemplate the unsearchable riches of divine mercy displayed in the Lord Jesus Christ.[4]

Meditation is one discipline that God longs for us to develop and one discipline that Satan longs for us to ignore. Through meditation on Scripture, we learn to distill God's voice from the many others that clamor for our attention. During times of silence, God may bring a certain verse to mind, bring a sense of peace over our being, or prick our hearts to intercede or pray for someone else. Though we most likely will not hear an audible voice, He will impress our minds, move our spirits, and touch our hearts. The Hebrew word for "meditate" is *hagah* and means "to utter or moan"...reflecting the sighing and low sounds one may make while musing, at least as the ancients practiced it.[5] "It was the habit of people reflecting on the Scriptures to turn the words over and over in their mind, and they did this by speaking the words, often in a whisper that sounded very much like mumbling. They would do this on an early morning walk, on a garden bench in the afternoon, or on their bed at night. Going over and over the words worked something like a root stimulator, allowing the words to penetrate their heart more quickly and more deeply."[6]

Making Room in Our Heart

Robert Boyd Munger, author of the booklet *My Heart Christ's Home*, described his relationship with Christ in terms of various rooms in a house. In it he wrote,

> Without question one of the most remarkable Christian doctrines is that Jesus Christ Himself through the presence of the Holy Spirit will actually enter a heart, settle down and be at home there. He [Jesus] came into the darkness of my heart and turned on the light. He built a fire in the cold hearth and banished the chill. He started music where there had been stillness and He filled the emptiness with His own loving wonderful fellowship.

Munger and Jesus strolled from room to room. They strolled into the library of his mind, the dining room of his appetites and desires, and the workshop of talents and skills. But the room that impacted him the greatest was the drawing room.

> We walked next into the drawing room. This room was rather intimate and comfortable. I liked it. It had a fireplace, overstuffed chairs, a bookcase, sofa, and a quiet atmosphere.
>
> He also seemed pleased with it. He said, "This is indeed a delightful room. Let us come here often. It is secluded and quiet and we can have fellowship together."
>
> Well, naturally, as a young Christian I was thrilled. I could not think of anything I would rather do than have a few minutes apart with Christ in intimate comradeship.
>
> He promised, "I will be here every morning early. Meet with Me here and we will start the day together." So morning after morning, I would come downstairs to the drawing room and He would take a book of the Bible...open it and then we would read together. He would tell me of its riches and unfold to me its truths...They were wonderful hours together. In fact, we called the drawing room the "withdrawing room." It was a period when we had our quiet time together.

But little by little, under the pressure of many responsibilities, this time began to be shortened...I began to miss a day now and then...I would miss it two days in a row and often more.

I remember one morning when I was in a hurry...As I passed the drawing room, the door was ajar. Looking in I saw a fire in the fireplace and the Lord sitting there..."Blessed Master, have You been here all these mornings?"

"Yes," He said, "I told you I would be here every morning to meet with you." Then I was even more ashamed. He had been faithful in spite of my faithlessness. I asked His forgiveness and He readily forgave me...

He said, "The trouble with you is this: You have been thinking of the quiet time, of the Bible study and prayer time, as a factor in your own spiritual progress, but you have forgotten that this hour means something to Me also."[7]

God created us to be in fellowship with Him. He longs for an intimate relationship with His children.

Do you remember that old picture that hung on many Sunday school walls years ago? It was a picture of Jesus standing at a door, knocking. The interesting thing about the door was that it had no handle on the outside. That wasn't a mistake by the artist. The door can only be opened from the inside. Jesus still knocks today, but He won't open the door and enter in on His own accord. He waits for us to invite Him in.

Let's Joust, Daddy!

In 1986 my husband and I built a house which we hoped to be our last stop before the retirement home. While the builders were hammering away, I was sewing away, trying to have all the curtains made before we moved in.

The fabric for the curtains came on five-foot-long cardboard tubes. For one year those tubes were my two-year-old son's favorite toys. They served as tunnels for Matchbox cars and giant megaphones from which all sorts of important announcements were made. But his favorite thing to do with the tubes was "joust." Every day when Steve came home from work, he was greeted by Steven shouting, "Let's joust, Daddy!" My husband jousted tirelessly for months.

Nine years later, in a conversation remembering the jousting days, Steven confessed, "You know, I used to have terrible nightmares about those huge cardboard tubes. When I was two, I used to dream that giant 'jousting rods' were chasing me all around the house trying to get me."

Baffled, I asked him, "Why didn't you tell us about the dreams then? And why did you want to continue to play with the tubes if they gave you bad dreams?"

He answered, "I guess it was because I loved Dad so much and playing the game with him, that it was worth having the scary dreams."

Little did Steven know what a profound statement he had just made. My thoughts immediately went to my heavenly Father, my love for Him, and what I was willing to endure to spend time with Him. I too have a jousting rod. It is called the "sword of the spirit, which is the word of God" (Ephesians 6:17). I love to joust with my heavenly Daddy. This jousting does not cause me to have bad dreams, but sometimes I have to endure a house that's not as clean as I would like or a project that is in the other room, screaming out to be finished. That's a nightmare to me.

In this busy world in which we live, taking time out to be with our Father can be somewhat of a struggle. But the rewards are great. So every morning I grab my jousting rod, God's Word, and say "Let's joust, Daddy." The only difference is that my Father and I are not fighting against each other, but side by side.

Preparing the Soil

I had a friend who discovered she had Hodgkin's disease. For one year Anita was housebound because of radiation and chemo treatments. I asked her, "Anita, what did you learn during those weeks and months when you were alone?"

She replied, "I learned how to recognize God's voice. When my daughter calls me on the phone, she never has to tell me, 'Hello, Mother. This is Heather.' Because I've spent so much time with her, I know her voice. That's how it is with God now. Over the past year, I've spent so much time with Him, I know His voice. I don't have to question if it is His or someone else's. When He speaks to me, I recognize His voice."

Oh, that each of us would have such an intimate relationship with Jesus Christ that we would recognize His voice completely. But that will not happen by osmosis. As with any intimate relationship, that level of open communication takes time. There are many who have accepted Christ as Savior, and have perhaps had faith in God for 30, 40, or 50 years, and yet have not sunk their spiritual roots deeply into the soil and become intimate with God. There are also many who have known Christ as Savior for a relatively short period of time, but know and commune with Him on such a personal level you can almost see them walking hand in hand. It's not a matter of the number of years we've been a Christian. It's a matter of the level of intimacy we've cultivated with Christ.

As we become women who listen to God, we must ask ourselves if we are willing to prepare our hearts to be receptive to His voice. Thomas Merton observed,

> Every moment and every event of every man's life on earth plants something in his soul. For just as the wind carries thousands of visible and invisible winged seeds, so the stream of time brings with it germs of spiritual vitality that come to rest imperceptibly in the minds and wills of men. Most of those unnumbered seeds perish and are lost, because men are not prepared to receive them.[8]

Jesus said much the same in His parable of the seeds. As we think about how to prepare our hearts to listen to God's voice, let's listen to Jesus' words recorded in Mark chapter 4, first to the multitudes and then to the disciples. I have written Jesus' words in bullet form to help us see His four points easily.

Listen! A farmer went out to sow his seed.

- As he was scattering the seed, some fell along the path, and birds came and ate it up.

- Some fell on rocky places, where it did not have much soil. It sprang up quickly, because the soil was shallow. But when the sun came up, the plants were scorched, and they withered because they had no root.

- Other seed fell among thorns, which grew up and choked the plants, so that they did not bear grain.

- Still other seed fell on good soil. It came up, grew and produced a crop, multiplying thirty, sixty, or even a hundred times.

Then Jesus said, "He who has ears to hear, let him hear" (Mark 4:3-9, emphasis added).

All through the Bible, God's words are referred to as seeds that are planted in our hearts. How we prepare the soil to receive those words can mean the difference between a spiritual wasteland or a fruitful field. This parable paints a portrait of four different hearts or four different types of soil. They lead us to ask questions about our own hearts.

Are our hearts hardened because of endless scurrying about that has packed the soil? Do seeds lie on the surface vulnerable to attack of spiritual vultures? Are they unable to penetrate the hard surface for the germination process to begin? If so, we need to "break up the fallow ground" so we can receive God's Word (Jeremiah 4:3; Hosea 10:12).

Are our hearts too shallow to allow the Word to take root deep within our souls? If so, we need to learn to meditate on God's Word and ask Him for a depth of soul and spirit that only the Holy Spirit can give.

Are our hearts too distracted by the cares of the world to focus on the things of God? Are the weeds of the world choking out God's voice? If so, we need to do a bit of soul-searching and spiritual gardening. Pull weeds of busyness, prune self-imposed demands, and trim the world's distractions (such as television).

And finally, are our hearts well prepared, freshly tilled, and expectantly receptive for the germination process to begin?

> Here is where the internalized seed begins its outward growth, changing our priorities and submitting them to Christ. Generally this doesn't happen overnight. It's a process of growth. When we give the Word of God space to live in our heart, the Spirit of God will cause it to take root, penetrating the earthiest recesses of our lives. Who can be sure how deeply its roots will burrow within us or how broadly its branches will extend beyond us? But if we give the Word space in the garden, of this we can be sure. The Holy Spirit will entwine the passage around the trellis of our life and apply it in ways we never could have imagined, vining its way not only to the lives of those around us but even to those down from us, across generations.[9]

Under Construction

In North Carolina, our state bird is the cardinal and the state flower is the dogwood. I have decided that our state shrub should be the orange-and-white construction barrel. Instead of our streets being lined with green helleri holly or red tip photinia bushes, many are donned with dunce-hat-shaped orange-and-white-striped plastic cones.

Our town of 300,000 had a growth spurt that took us to 500,000 in what seemed like the twinkling of an eye. And like that adolescent boy who suddenly has pants that are too short and ears that are too big, our community had schools that were too small and roads that were too narrow.

My family lived on the outskirts of town to avoid the hubbub of the inner city. But before long, the outskirts became the "inskirts" and our quiet neighborhood, with a spine and six cul-de-sacs branching off to the left and right, became surrounded by major arteries, pumping cars around our quiet suburban lives. Pretty soon the arteries had a bad case of arteriosclerosis due to too much motor oil.

My son's school was just five minutes from our home—at 10:00 A.M., that is. At 7:30 A.M. the main road to the school became the road most traveled, and our trek became a 30- to 35-minute Oregon Trail experience. Our little two-lane road was definitely over-worked and under-paved!

During Steven's second-grade year we saw a city truck come and line the road with orange-and-white-striped cone-shaped construction barrels. It was then we knew that this street was about to have triple bypass surgery. I didn't know if I should be happy or sad. I knew construction would mean a smoother ride in the future, but a slower ride in the present.

Bulldozers came and dug up one side of the road and turned the two lanes into one. Now we're talking congestive heart failure—mine that is. I tried to have a good attitude about the bumpy road ahead, but after a few months my attitude began to take a turn for the worse.

"I can't stand this dust." "I can't stand this mud." "Mommy, why does it take three men to hold the flag?" "Mommy, why are those ten men lying over in the grass and only two are working?" "Mrs. Jaynes, there's nothing wrong with your car. You just have four bent tire rims from running over potholes." Besides, orange is such an ugly color.

Then one day, two and a half years after the emergence of the despised orange barrels and construction signs (these guys gave new meaning to "slow men working"), a wonderful young man in a beautiful white truck came by and one-by-one lifted the eyesores onto his flat bed and hauled these plastic cones away. Did I say away? Actually, he picked up the ugly things, turned the corner and put them down on another one of the main arteries that we traveled each day. This signaled that we were in for two more years of dust, broken pavement, and flagmen. Warning! Road Construction Ahead! Maybe "Bring Out the Barrels, We'll Have a Barrel of Fun" should be our state song.

No one likes road construction (except maybe flagmen, barrel manufacturers, and asphalt factories). Likewise, I certainly don't get excited when the Lord comes by and plops an orange-and-white barrel down on some aspect of my life that needs an overhaul. Becoming a woman who listens to God is a process, and from now until I see Jesus face-to-face, I will be a woman under construction. I would love to live on easy street, but more often than not, bulldozers are digging up one of my lanes and causing upheaval in my life. I have inner potholes and cracked pavement that need repairing, and instead of easy street, it's usually the road of hard knocks. I like the finished product, but I detest the work in progress.

Now when I see those orange barrels, I thank the Lord for His continuous work on my life. I am grateful when He sees fit to clear the roads or redirect my path. But I look forward to the day when I walk through those pearly gates and see the streets all clean and glistening in the Son light, paved not with the asphalt of my humanity, but with the gold of Christ's glory. There'll be no more construction barrels in sight, and the way will be clear for me to praise Him for all eternity.

SIXTEEN

Blessings of Listening to God

JAKE WAS JUST A SIMPLE COUNTRY BOY from Robeson County in eastern North Carolina. His parents were so proud of their son when he was accepted at the prestigious Duke University, which stands as a bastion of higher learning and intellect. Gothic buildings with English ivy clinging to walls of stone, mature boxwood hedges hemming in profuse flower gardens, and 100-year-old oak trees shading rolling green hills all combine to create a distinctly European feel in the middle of Durham, North Carolina.

During the fall of Jake's freshman year, he attended a Campus Crusade for Christ meeting and heard the gospel presented in a way he had never heard before. That very night, Jake eagerly made a total and complete commitment to Jesus Christ, and God forever changed his life. All through his freshman year, Jake studied the Bible, learned how to pray, and observed his mentors share the gospel with students all around the campus.

When Jake was a sophomore, he and a group of other Christian friends requested an audience with an on-campus fraternity, and Jake was chosen to share his testimony.

"I entered that frat house with fear and trepidation," Jake said. "You never knew what those guys were going to do. They might laugh, listen, or leave. But I stood up in front of those upper-classmen and told them about how Jesus had changed my life the year before. Afterward, a friend of mine handed out index cards and asked them to write down what they thought about the presentation or to note if they wanted to know more about the gospel. Mike was one who said, 'I want to know more.'

"The next day, a senior and I made an appointment to meet with Mike. I was basically going along to pray and observe. However, on the day of the appointment, my friend became ill. I didn't want to pass up the opportunity to meet with Mike, so I decided to go alone."

Of course, Jake wasn't alone. Jesus was right there with him, orchestrating the entire meeting. I imagine there was a battle going on in Jake's mind—conflicting voices telling him to go and to stay at home, he could do it and he couldn't, he was ready and he wasn't. Jake determined which voice was God's and decided to keep the appointment.

Jake whispered a prayer and walked into Mike's tiny single-man dorm room. In one corner, Mike, a robust 6′2″ college senior, sat in a seemingly ominous black leather recliner that took up one-third of the room. As Jake sat on the edge of the bed, questions began to flood his mind. *Who am I to witness to this intelligent premed student? I've only been a Christian for one year. Suppose he asks me questions I can't answer? Maybe I shouldn't have come alone.* But instead of listening to his fears and running, Jake listened to God and stayed.

"What did you think about the meeting the other night? What is your perception of God? Have you ever heard of the four spiritual laws?"

Jake pulled out a small booklet and shared four simple truths with Mike.

1. God loves you and offers a wonderful plan for your life.

2. But man is sinful and separated from God and cannot experience God's plan for his life.

3. Jesus Christ is God's only provision for man's sin.

   4. You must accept Christ as Savior and Lord to experience
      God's plan for your life.[1]

   Then Jake asked, "Mike, do you think this is something you
would like to do?"

   Within minutes, the two young men were on their knees and
Jake Cane ushered Mike into the kingdom of Christ. Over the next
year, Mike asked Jake to teach him everything he knew about how
to have a personal and ongoing relationship with Jesus. Jake
began as a student, became a disciple, then an evangelist, and
finally began to disciple others. After a few years, Jake graduated
from Duke and moved to Chicago to attend Trinity Evangelical
School. Mike went on to medical school at Duke to pursue his
dream of becoming a physician.

   Years passed and the young men lost touch. One night Jake
received a call from his mother informing him that his father was
dying from the kidney disease that had plagued his life for several
years. He had been transported to the Veterans' Hospital across the
street from Duke Medical Center. Jake quickly caught a plane to see
his dad, who was on peritoneal dialysis and suffering from uremic
poisoning.

   While Jake's dad had been a moral man, he had never come to
saving faith in Jesus Christ. More than for his physical health, Jake
wrestled in prayer for his dad's spiritual life. Jake knew his father
was no longer lucid. He didn't recognize anyone and was unable
to respond to those around him. Thus, Jake felt his opportunity to
witness to his father one last time was lost.

   At 2:00 A.M Jake sat alone in the dimly lit waiting room of the
intensive care unit of the VA hospital. The chilly room was in the
basement with no windows and no signs of life. He felt alone,
numb, and helpless. Suddenly, a man's approaching footsteps tapping against the linoleum floor interrupted the silence. Jake
looked up and saw a doctor in a white lab coat walking toward
him. When the man came close enough for Jake to see his face,
he stared in disbelief.

"Jake, is that you?" the man said.

"Mike! What are you doing here?"

The two men embraced like long-lost brothers.

"I have a patient in this unit," Mike said. "Last week I witnessed to him and he accepted Christ. I heard he wasn't doing very well, so I thought I'd come by and check on him."

"What's the patient's name?" Jake asked.

"Thomas Cane," he answered slowly, letting the full ramification of his answer sink in.

"That's my dad," Jake said with tears in his eyes.

At that very moment, alarms rang signaling a code blue, and Jake's father left this world and entered into the heavenly throne room to spend eternity with his Savior.

In 1971, a young college sophomore listened and obeyed God, and introduced an aspiring premed student to Jesus Christ. Six years later, a young doctor led that same man's dying father to saving faith. You may never know the impact of listening to God. As Jake told me, "I cast my bread on the water and it came back to me. In this case, it came back buttered."

Blessings of Obedience

Oswald Chambers, author of the classic book *My Utmost for His Highest*, wrote,

> If you yourself do not cut the lines that tie you to the dock, God will have to use a storm to sever them and to send you out to sea...Put everything in your life afloat upon God, going out to sea on the great swelling tide of His purpose, and your eyes will be opened...When you know that you should do something and you do it, immediately you know more. Examine where you have become sluggish, where you began losing interest spiritually, and you will find that it goes back to a point where you did not do something you knew you should.[2]

The simple fact is that when we listen and obey, God will speak more often and give us more opportunities to serve Him.

Jesus plainly said, "Whoever has my commands and obeys them, he is the one who loves me" (John 14:21). James reiterated his brother's words, "Do not merely listen to the word, and so deceive yourselves. Do what it says" (James 1:22). Intimacy with God begins with listening to His voice, but the relationship bursts into full bloom when we move to obey.

I am always touched by Mary's humble acceptance of and obedience to God's will for her life. The angel Gabriel came to Mary and told her that she, being a virgin, would be with child, give birth to God's Son, and name Him Jesus. He explained that the Holy Spirit would come upon her and the power of the Most High would overshadow her in an immaculate conception. Mary didn't argue, didn't complain, or give all the reasons why this was going to ruin her reputation and her future. She simply replied, "I am the Lord's servant. May it be done to me as you have said" (Luke 1:38). It should come as no surprise that 33 years later, when she and her Son were at a wedding feast in Cana and the host ran out of wine, she turned to the servants and said, "Whatever he [Jesus] says to you, do it" (John 2:5 NASB). She had learned the lesson and blessing of obedience from the Master Himself.

Once again, Oswald Chambers wrote,

> All God's revelations are sealed until they are opened to us by obedience. You will never open them through philosophy or thinking. But once you obey, a flash of light comes immediately...Obey God in the thing He shows you, and instantly the next thing is opened up...God will never reveal more truth about Himself until you have obeyed what you already know.[3]

We must never fall into the trap of thinking that God will always give us "big" things to do. "Jesus...wrapped a towel around his waist...and began to wash his disciples' feet..." (John 13:3-5). Through His act of servant leadership, He demonstrated the obedience we should have on a daily basis in the mundane activities of everyday life. Yes, He raised the dead, but He also washed the disciples' feet.

One evening Steve and I were on our way to dinner. Just before we arrived, I saw three teenage girls walking into another restaurant in the same area where we were going to eat. One of the girls had been in a small group I had led for two years. I felt God nudging me to go into the restaurant and pay for their dinners.

"Steve, there's Christine," I said. "I believe God wants me to pay for those girls' dinners."

Steve, being a man who listens to God, whipped the car around and drove me to the door of the other restaurant.

"Hi, girls," I said as I walked up to them in line.

"Hi, Mrs. Jaynes. What are you doing here?"

"May I take your order?" the cashier interrupted.

"Go ahead, girls," I urged.

Each girl ordered and then the cashier turned to me. "And you, ma'am?"

"Oh, I'm not having anything. I just came in to pay for these girls' dinners."

The threesome were very surprised and very appreciative. I ran back out to our car, feeling a warm sense of listening and obeying.

The next day, Christine called. "Mrs. Jaynes," she said "thank you so much for paying for our dinners last night. My friends were so touched. No one has ever done anything like that for any of us before. See, last night, they wanted to go out to dinner, but I told them I couldn't afford it. So they were going to pay for mine. Then you came in and well...thanks."

Listening and obeying God's gentle nudge only cost me $19.95, but the lesson to Christine and her two friends was invaluable. Jesus said, "Give, and it will be given to you. A good measure, pressed down, shaken together and running over, will be poured into your lap. For with the measure you use, it will be measured to you" (Luke 6:38).

Obeying God begins with heeding the simple nudges. Don't be afraid! Many people are afraid to obey those nudges because they aren't absolutely sure it is God's voice. I've decided that if the inner prompting lines up with Scripture and is consistent with God's character and ways, then I'd rather err on the side of obedience than the side of caution.

By nature, I am a fairly organized person. When I am invited to speak at a women's conference, I begin preparing weeks or months in advance. However, there have been times when God has completely interrupted my plans and given me a message at the last minute. When this happens, I've learned to put my well-organized, neatly categorized, concisely conceptualized notes and handouts aside.

At one retreat, I had planned four sessions and the outlines had been sent ahead weeks in advance. But the night before, as I was reviewing my notes, God very clearly told me I was to share a different message. Did I argue? You bet. *(I've already sent my outlines.)* Did I try to talk Him out of it? Yes, indeed. *(But, Lord, this was such a good message.)* Did I obey? Eventually.

The first session, on Friday night, I spoke according to my plan. I had a fitful night's sleep, if I slept at all. He kept nudging and, to be honest, the nudges started to be a bit painful as He poked the same spot of my heart over and over again.

The next morning I told the ladies that God had another message for them other than what was on their outlines. They put their papers away, I put my notes away, and I opened my mouth as God opened their hearts. Just two days before, God had spoken to me about my childhood dreams. The first was the dream I had to have a daddy who loved me. My father was a workaholic who had bouts of heavy drinking and violent outbursts. Very rarely, if ever, did he show any type of affection toward me when I was a child. God took me to scripture after scripture that showed me He was my heavenly Father who fulfilled every longing of my little girl heart.

I had also dreamed of being a bride and even practiced the wedding march down my parents' long hallway. Even though I have a wonderful husband, God took me to passage after passage showing me how I was the bride of Christ. He showed me how the Old Testament fathers chose a bride for their sons, paid a price for her, left her gifts, and then went away for the son to build a house for her. The groom-to-be couldn't return until the father said the house was ready. God showed me that He chose me as the bride for His Son and paid a very high price for me (Christ's blood). The groom has left gifts for me (gifts of the Spirit) and is now away preparing our home. He will return when His Father tells Him the house is ready for His bride.

A third dream I had as a little girl was to be a mommy with a house full of children. After the birth of my son, Steven, my husband and I traveled down the painful road of infertility: poking, prodding, and timed intimacy. During that time, we did conceive, but we lost the child due to a miscarriage. It became evident that Steven was to be an only child. As I was reading about being the bride of Christ in Song of Solomon, God struck me with Song of Solomon 2:2 NASB, "I am the Rose of Sharon."

"What's your name, child," He seemed to say.

"Sharon," I answered aloud.

"Look it up," He continued.

When I looked up Sharon in my Bible dictionary, I learned that it was a *fertile valley*. God spoke to my heart. *On your medical chart, there is the word "infertile." However, I made sure your name was fertile from the beginning of time. You do not have a houseful of children that have been born in your womb, but you have a heartful of children that have been born through your ministry.*

There were three dreams of a woman that God revealed to me that day. And while it went against every organized bone in my body, it was the message I gave those women in Georgia. It was a powerful presentation—not because of me, but because I was obedient and listened to a powerful God! That message, *Dreams of a Woman: God's Plan for Fulfilling Your Dream*, is now a book published by Focus on the Family. I wonder what would have happened had I turned a deaf ear?

Sometimes you get to see the rewards of listening to God and sometimes you may never know the outcome. One day I bought a beautiful bouquet of miniature roses from the grocery store. As I walked to my car, I saw a woman struggling with her two-year-old and newborn. When I engaged in conversation with her, she shared this was her first trip out of the house since her baby had been born.

Immediately, God nudged me to give her my roses. There was a bit of a struggle. (They were, after all, the last bunch in the store.) Thankfully, obedience won out.

"Here are some flowers for you. God wants you to have them. Have a great day." And then like Zorro, I hopped in my car and disappeared. No thanks. No fanfare. No applause. Just a warm feeling in my heart which had a strong resemblance to a holy hug.

I wish I could tell you that I've listened and obeyed every time I've heard God's voice or felt His nudge, but I haven't. There have been many times when I planted my feet and turned a deaf ear. But in retrospect, I wonder how many blessings I missed because I've refused to listen to His voice and reap the rewards of obedience.

> We all have those times when there are no flashes of light and no apparent thrill to life, where we experience nothing but the daily routine with its common everyday tasks...Don't always expect God to give you His thrilling moments, but learn to live in those common times of the drudgery of life by the power of God....I must realize that my obedience even in the smallest detail of life has all the omnipotent power of the grace of God behind it.[4]

> If I obey Jesus Christ in the seemingly random circumstances of life, they become pinholes through which I see the face of God.[5]

Throughout the pages of *Becoming a Woman Who Listens to God*, I have shared stories of how God has spoken to me in my everyday life. The stories are meant to do more than bring a smile or even perhaps a tear. They are meant to touch your heart. That's what Jesus did while here on earth. That's what He still does today.

As I read through the Old Testament, I see God's appeal to mankind was through principles, commandments, and laws. But then, as I turn the page from Malachi 4:6 to Matthew 1:1, there seems to be a shift—and it all began with the cry of a baby in a manger.

In the New Testament, Jesus told stories or parables because His appeal was and is to our hearts. Yes, God still wants us to obey His commands, but He longs for us to obey because we love Him and not simply out of a sense of duty.

Jesus was the smartest man who ever lived. Have you ever thought about that? The smartest. Ever. And yet He spoke to us with stories. Oh, He could have given us more principles or laws to follow, but in earnest, He gave very few. "Love the Lord your God with all your heart...Love your neighbor as yourself" (Matthew 22:37,39). He told the Pharisee who inquired which was the greatest commandment.

There are great blessings awaiting you as you listen to the stories that God reveals through each page of your life. Remember the "Where's Waldo" books? In each busy picture would be hidden a lanky man with a red-and-white-striped hat. It was fun to try and find Waldo on every page. I can tell you, it's even more fun to look for Jesus on each page of our lives.

The Winner

It was the first swim meet of the year for our newly formed middle school aquatics team. The atmosphere on the three-hour bus ride was electric with anticipation as the band of 48 adolescents thought of nothing but victory. However, the electricity turned into shock as our minnows filed off the bus and stared in disbelief at their muscle-clad, Neptunelike opponents.

The coach checked the schedule. *Surely there's been a mistake,* he thought. But the schedule only confirmed that, yes, this was the right place and the right time.

The two teams formed a line on the side of the pool. Whistles blew, races were begun, and races were lost. Halfway through the meet, Coach Huey realized he had no participants for one of the events.

"Okay, team, who wants to swim the 500-yard freestyle?" the coach asked.

Several hands shot up, including Justin's. "I'll race, Coach!"

The coach looked down at the freckle-faced youth and said, "Justin, this race is 20 lengths of the pool. I've only seen you swim eight."

"Oh, I can do it, Coach. Let me try. What's 12 more laps?"

The coach reluctantly conceded. *After all,* he thought, *it's not the winning but the trying that builds character.*

The whistle blew and the opponents torpedoed through the water and finished the race in a mere four minutes and fifty seconds. The winners gathered on the sidelines to socialize while our group struggled to finish. After four more long minutes, the last exhausted members of our team emerged from the water. The last except for Justin.

Justin was stealing breaths as his hands slapped against the water and pushed it aside to propel his thin body forward. It appeared that he would go under at any minute, yet something seemed to keep pushing him onward.

"Why doesn't the coach stop this child?" the parents whispered among themselves. "He looks like he's about to drown, and the race was won four minutes ago."

But what the parents did not realize was that the real race, the race of a boy becoming a man, was just beginning.

The coach walked over to the young swimmer, knelt down and quietly spoke.

Relieved parents thought, "Oh, he's finally going to pull that boy out before he kills himself."

But to their surprise, the coach rose from the concrete, stepped back from the pool's edge, and the young man continued to swim.

One teammate, inspired by his brave friend, went to the side of the pool and walked the lane as Justin pressed on. "Come on, Justin, you can do it! You can do it! Keep going! Don't give up!"

He was joined by another, then another, until the entire team was walking the length of the pool rooting for and encouraging their fellow swimmer to finish the race set before him.

The opposing team saw what was happening and joined the chant. The students' contagious chorus sent a chill through the room and soon the once-concerned parents were on their feet cheering, shouting, and praying. The room was pulsating with energy and excitement as teammates and opponents alike pumped courage into one small swimmer.

Twelve long minutes after the starting whistle had blown, an exhausted but smiling Justin swam his final lap and struggled to pull himself out the pool. The crowd had applauded the first swimmer as he crossed the line in first place. But they gave Justin the greater cheer for finishing the race.

In 2 Timothy 4:7, Paul writes, "I have fought the good fight, I have finished the race, I have kept the faith." On some days, when the swimming or running grows difficult—on those days when I want to quit—I long for friends and family who will walk the course with me cheering me on. "Come on, Sharon, you can do it!" "Don't give up! You're almost there!"

But I know there will be many days that I will look around and discover there is no one there to cheer me on. That's when I need to look a bit closer, listen a bit more intently, and hear the still small voice of my heavenly Father. He's always there to pick me up when I fall, hold me when I cry, hug me when I'm feeling alone, cheer for me when I'm victorious, and love me when I'm just me. Our heavenly Parent is cheering for you too, my friend. He's saying, "Keep going! Don't give up! You are precious to Me! You're not alone! You can do it!"

Shhh. Can you hear it? That still small voice of love.

Oh, the joys of becoming a woman who listens to God. There's no sweeter sound I know.

STANDING AT THE CROSSROADS

❦

y prayer for each new day is that I will be able to say like the prophet Isaiah, "He wakens me morning by morning, wakens my ear to listen like one being taught. The Sovereign LORD has opened my ears, and I have not been rebellious; I have not drawn back" (Isaiah 50:4-5).

> Whether it means life or death—it makes no difference! (Philippians 1:21). Paul was determined that nothing would stop him from doing exactly what God wanted. But before we choose to follow God's will, a crisis must develop in our lives. We stand at the crossroads of whether to listen to God's gentle nudges or ignore them. This happens because we tend to be unresponsive to God's gentler nudges. He brings us to the place where He asks us to be our utmost for Him and we begin to debate. He then providentially produces a crisis where we have to decide for or against. The moment becomes a great crossroads in our lives. If a crisis has come to you on any front, surrender your will to Jesus absolutely and irrevocably.[1]

I have stood at that crossroads many times in my life, but perhaps the most defining time was when I decided to obey God's call on my life to be involved with Proverbs 31 Ministries. For many years I had been writing devotionals and stories but shared them with no one. I stuffed them in a drawer and held them tightly as my little secrets between God and me. But then God spoke to my heart and told me He didn't want the stories to be our little secret. He had entrusted me with treasures that were meant to be shared, not hidden away. But what was He calling me to do? I had an inkling, but it didn't make sense. My college degree was in dental hygiene, and it made no sense for someone with a math and science degree to write books or become a conference speaker. But I continued to read His Word and pray for the Holy Spirit to reveal what He was calling me to do. I also watched what God was doing in and around me and paid close attention to my circumstances.

Over the next year, I cleared my plate of various "servings" that were cluttering my ability to hear God clearly. I committed to pray about where God was leading me. It was as if I had the introduction to this new call written in my mind, but had no idea what the title or the content of the first chapter would be.

In the meantime, there was a young woman who was diligently working in a new ministry for women, Proverbs 31 Ministries. She knew that she could not do it alone, and began to pray that God would send her a ministry partner with the same passion and vision for touching women's hearts and building godly homes. Almost one year to the date of her first prayer, Lysa TerKeurst and I met for a radio interview. I was her guest, sharing several of my devotional stories and information on how to reach out to women experiencing infertility. When the interview was over, Lysa told me she had been praying for a ministry partner and felt as though God was telling her it was me. Very doubtful, I thanked her and half-heartedly agreed to pray about it.

If you have read any of my other books, the following story will be familiar to you, but I cannot effectively share my journey of becoming a woman who listens to God without including it. A few weeks after my initial invitation from Lysa, my husband and I went on a romantic getaway to Bermuda. Here's what happened while we were there....

Lame Man Dancing

One summer my husband and I escaped to the captivating island of Bermuda, where the water is crystal clear and the bluest of blues and the air is filled with the scent of blooming hibiscus. The vacation was complete with long romantic walks on white sandy beaches, splashing waves on limestone rock jetties, and discoveries of secluded ocean-carved caves. At night, a million tiny green Bermuda tree frogs sang romantic cadences just for us.

On one particular evening, Steve and I went on a dining adventure to a five-star restaurant filled with men and women dressed in their very finest evening apparel. The semicircular dining room was lined with glass, overlooked the Atlantic Ocean and allowed the flaming orange-red of the setting sun to be our backdrop.

In one corner of the dining area, a four-man orchestra filled the room with fluid sounds of music from the '40s and '50s. Steve wanted to see if we could remember the steps from our ballroom dance lessons. "Come on, Sharon," he urged. "Let's go take a spin on the dance floor and see if we can remember the fox-trot."

"No way," I replied, "Nobody else is out there. I'm not going to be the only one on the floor with everyone staring at me. And suppose we mess up? I'd be embarrassed. It's been a long time since we've danced, and I don't remember all the steps. Let's wait until there are some other people dancing. Then I'll go."

Finally the first couple approached the floor. They looked like professional dancers, moving as one and never missing a beat. This did not encourage me at all, but only strengthened my resolve that this was no place for my feet to tread.

Then couple number one was joined by couple number two, whose steps weren't quite as perfect.

"Okay, now I'll go," I agreed. "But let's go get in the back corner where nobody can see us."

So off we went to our little spot on the wooden dance floor and tried to remember the 1-2-3-4s of the fox-trot. As we were moving as two, I noticed a fourth couple approach the floor. They came with confidence—no hesitation, no timidity. But there was something very special about this couple. The man was in a wheelchair.

He was a middle-aged, slightly balding, large-framed man with a neatly trimmed beard. On his left hand he wore a white glove, I guessed to cover a skin disease. Both were dressed in evening wear, but the most beautiful part of their dress was the radiant smiles they were both wearing. Their love for each other lit up the room.

As the band played a peppy beat, the wife held her love's healthy right hand and danced with him. He never did rise from the wheelchair that had become his legs, but they didn't seem to care. They came together and separated like expert dancers. He spun her around as she stooped to conform to her husband's seated position. Lovingly, like a little fairy child, she danced around his chair while his laughter became the fifth instrument in this small orchestra. Even though his feet did not move from their metal resting place, his shoulders swayed in perfect time and his eyes danced with hers.

My heart was so moved by this love story unfolding before my eyes that I had to turn my head and bury my face on Steve's shoulder so no one would see the tears streaming down my cheeks. As I did, I saw every person in this rigid, formal dining room had tears trickling down their cheeks. All around the room linen napkins were dabbing tearful eyes. Even the band was transfixed by this portrait of love and devotion.

Then the music slowed to a lazy romantic melody. The wife pulled a chair up beside her husband but facing in the opposite direction, and they held in a dancers' embrace. One arm was extended as the other was placed on her love's shoulder. Cheek to cheek they swayed to the piano man's romantic love song. At one point they both closed their eyes, and I imagined, dreamed of an earlier time when they were not restrained by his chair.

After watching this incredible display of love and courage, I realized that my inhibitions of not wanting others to watch me because my steps were not perfect were gone. The Lord spoke to my heart in a powerful way.

Sharon, I want you to notice who moved this crowd to tears. Was it couple number one, with their perfect steps? Or, was it the last couple, who not only did not have perfect steps, but had no steps at all? No, My child, it was the display of love, not perfection, that had an effect on the people watching. If you obey Me, I will do it for you just as his wife did it for him.

For some time I had been praying about whether to answer God's call to become one of the voices of the radio arm of Proverbs 31 Ministries. I had argued with the Lord, telling Him that I was not qualified—that I was not "good enough" to serve. I assured Him He had made a mistake in choosing me. But just as He answered Moses' arguments, God answered mine. He said, "I will do it for you."

My steps will never be perfect, on a dance floor or, more importantly, in life. But the Lord doesn't expect my steps to be perfect. He just expects me to listen to His voice, to be obedient, to take the first step of faith, and to let Him do the rest. The man in the wheelchair never even moved his feet, but his wife did the moves for him. And I need to remember that the Lord will do the same for me. I also need to remember that it is not perfect steps that the world is so desperately looking for. They aren't impressed by perfect people who live in perfect houses with perfect children. They are impressed by love. Genuine, God-inspired love. That's what moves a crowd.

That night, by the beautiful shores of Bermuda, the Lord sent a lame man to teach me how to dance.

Listening to Your Story

When my son was young, we played a game called "tell me a story." Whether we were riding in the car, or I was giving him a bath or helping him clean up his room, "tell me a story" was one of his favorite pastimes. Steven made up the first line of a story, and then it was my job to weave a tale. "Once upon a time there was a leaf," he'd say. "Once upon a time there was a lizard..." "Once upon a time there was a dog named Fido..." "Once upon a time there was a boy..." Some scenarios were more difficult to craft than others, and each was unique.

I'm inviting you to listen to a story, only I'm not the one weaving the tale. God is. God speaks to us through the Bible, through the Holy Spirit, through prayer, through other people, through our circumstances, and through nature. He wants to speak to you through the pages of your life—only it's no fairy tale. You get to write the first line and then sit back and let God weave an intricate story of mercy and grace and love. "Once upon a time there was a girl named...(your name).

Can You Hear Him?

When I was a small child, I remember sitting in a sparsely decorated Sunday school room and musing over a solitary picture of Jesus that hung on the stark white wall. In this picture, Jesus stood peacefully knocking at someone's door. I can remember wondering, *Why is He knocking? Isn't He God? Why doesn't He just walk on in?* I surmised that Jesus must have been a gentleman who would never rush in where He wasn't welcome. I also daydreamed about who lived on the other side of that door. Was it a family like my own, with a mommy, daddy, and two children? Or was it perhaps a grandma, who lived alone and waited anxiously for someone to stop by for a visit?

Other questions have occurred to me since: *Is anyone home? What kind of house would Jesus visit? What would it be like to open your front door and find Jesus standing there?* Throughout my life, God has given me glimpses of the varied doors upon which He knocks: a motorcyclist at an amusement park, a crying baby in a grocery store, a weary mother with no more to give, a prisoner in Alcatraz, a young woman dying of cancer.

Let me share one final story with you about God's gentle whisper and Jesus' loving knock. It all started in a small southeastern town many years ago, in a tranquil North Carolina neighborhood. A little girl lived with her mommy, daddy, and one older brother. Their ranch-style house with rounded columns, smoky blue shutters, and welcoming red door was surrounded by a canopy of 30-foot pine trees. Pink and white azaleas and an immaculate lawn portrayed a picture of tranquility and peace, but inside the walls of her home, the atmosphere brewed with hostility and fear.

Her father was a successful businessman who spent little time with the family. When he was home, he drank heavily, and her parents fought both verbally and physically in her presence. Many nights she would lie in bed with the covers pulled tightly under her chin, praying she would quickly fall asleep to shut out the sound of her parents' fighting and yelling. On several occasions, she would slip out of her bed at night, tiptoe over to her pink ballerina jewelry box, and wind the key in the back. Then she would open the lid of the box and place her ear close to the music box in an effort to shut out the sound of her parents arguing in the next room. Her parents did indeed love the child, but because they were so miserable with themselves and their marriage, they had a hard time knowing how to express that love.

When she was 12 years old, the little girl, who was no longer so little, began spending a lot of time with her friend, Wanda Henderson. Wanda's mother took the child under her wing and loved her as though she were her own. Mrs. Henderson knew about the home with its broken lives and occasional broken furniture. And she knew about the girl's broken heart.

Mr. and Mrs. Henderson had a great marriage. They hugged and kissed each other in front of the children, and even called each other by pet names. For the first time in her life, the girl saw what a relationship between husband and wife was supposed to be like. She didn't understand all the reasons why the Hendersons' home was so full of love and so strikingly different from her own, but she knew that the difference had something to do with Jesus Christ. Perhaps it was their witness. Perhaps it was God's voice. Most likely it was both.

One day Mrs. Henderson asked if the girl would like to attend church with her family and she quickly agreed. She had attended church before, but the people in the Hendersons' church were different. She noticed that they had more than a religion—they had a relationship with Jesus and talked about Him as though they knew Him personally. The next year, Mrs. Henderson started a Bible study for teens and the girl never missed a meeting, devouring every word. Then one night, when the girl was 14, Mrs. Henderson asked her if she was ready to accept Jesus Christ as her personal Savior. She remembered a picture of Jesus that she had seen hanging on the stark white wall of her Sunday school class some ten years earlier—a picture of Jesus standing at a door, knocking, and waiting patiently to come in. She realized at that moment, the door was indeed the door of her heart.

So that night, the young girl opened the door and welcomed Jesus into her heart, and He forever changed her life. In case you haven't guessed, that little girl was me. Three years later, my mother became a Christian and two years after that, my father committed his life to the Lord. I finally had the family my heart had always longed for. I've never gotten over the wonder of what can happen when you open a door. A whole new world could be waiting.

Jesus still knocks on doors. Perhaps He's knocking on yours. Maybe you invited Him in years ago, but as the house got cluttered, you ran out of time to pay attention to His voice or, wanting to pursue activities not to His liking, you pushed Him out of the door. Now as He knocks, what will you say? Why not welcome Him to cross the threshold of your heart? Shhhh. Can you hear it? He's knocking still.

"Here I am! I stand at the door and knock. If anyone hears my voice and opens the door, I will come in and eat with him, and he with me" (Revelation 3:20).

A Tune-Up for Listening to God

Chapter 1—God Speaks Through His Word

A Closer Look at God's Word

Psalm 119 is a storehouse of powerful verses about God's Word and how He speaks to us through Scripture.

1. Read the following verses and note what you learn about God's Word.

   a. verse 4

   b. verse 11

   c. verse 14

   d. verse 74

   e. verse 105

2. Read the following verses and note how the psalmist felt about God's Word.

   a. verse 16

    b. verse 20

    c. verse 40

    d. verse 42

    e. verse 47

    f. verse 52

    g. verse 81

    h. verse 97

3. Write five words describing how you feel about God's Word.

4. What was the psalmist's prayer regarding God's Word?

    a. verse 18

    b. verse 26

    c. verse 27

    d. verse 28

    e. verse 133

5. Try your hand at penning a prayer regarding God speaking to you through His Word.

6. What comes to those who love God's Word? (verse 165)

7. What do you learn from Luke 24:44 about why the disciples finally understood the Scriptures? How does this relate to the way we should approach Scripture and our prayer for illumination?

Chapter 2—God Speaks Through the Holy Spirit

The Holy Spirit Brings Power

1. What was John the Baptist's prediction about the type of baptism Jesus would bring? (John 1:33)

2. What did Jesus tell the disciples regarding the Holy Spirit in Acts 1:4?

3. What did Jesus tell them would be the outcome of the baptism of the Holy Spirit? (Acts 1:8)

4. Look up the word "witness" in a dictionary. Define.

5. Read the account of the coming of the Holy Spirit upon the disciples in Acts 2. What was the initial manifestation of those filled with the Holy Spirit? (2:6-8) How does this confirm Jesus' stated purpose for the baptism of the Holy Spirit?

6. Read Acts 4:23-29. What was their request?

7. There were two results to those who observed the coming of the Holy Spirit. What were they? (Acts 2:4; Acts 2:41) What does this say to you?

8. Compare the Peter we see in John 18:15-27 to the Peter we see in Acts 2:14-41. How was he different?

9. What promise does Peter give us in Acts 2:38-39?

10. Where does the Holy Spirit dwell? (Romans 8:9; 1 Corinthians 6:19)

11. Read Acts 4:13 below. Put your name in the verse: When they saw the courage of (your name), and they realized that she was an ordinary woman, they were astonished and they took note that she had been with Jesus!

Chapter 3—God Speaks Through Prayer

Nehemiah—A Man of Prayer

1. Read Nehemiah chapter 1. What was the situation in Jerusalem?

2. Note that the first thing Nehemiah did when he heard the news was to go to God in prayer. Give several highlights of Nehemiah's prayer.

3. How was Nehemiah's second prayer in 2:4 different from his first lengthy prayer? What do you think this prayer sounded like in his mind?

4. How do you think Nehemiah came up with the plan to rebuild the walls of Jerusalem? (Nehemiah 2:11-12)

5. What was the reaction of the majority? (2:17-18; 4:6)

6. Scan Nehemiah 3 and note the organization of his building plan. Also, note his previous occupation in 2:1. How do you think he had the skill and wisdom to set up such an intricate plan?

7. Was everyone happy with Nehemiah's plan? (2:19-20; 4:1-3) Have you ever proceeded in a situation when you felt you had heard from God but faced opposition? Explain.

8. What was Nehemiah's reaction to the opposition? (4:4-5,7-9) What should be our reaction to opposition?

9. Did the Jews' courage wane at times? (4:10-14) Do you think fatigue played a part in their doubting? What can we learn from this?

10. How did Nehemiah get the Jews to refocus during their time of doubting? (4:14-18)

11. After the project was complete, what did the people do? (Nehemiah 8:10) Write out the last half of verse 10.

12. We can learn a lot from Nehemiah, a man who listened to God. List five lessons God has shown you as you've read Nehemiah's story.

Chapter 4—God Speaks Through Circumstances

Priceless Personal Parables

Jesus said, "Anyone who has seen me has seen the Father" (John 14:9). Read about the following set of circumstances and record what you learn about God's character and His ways through Jesus' actions. For example: God loves children and never sees them as an interruption, or God has control over nature.

1. Matthew 8:1-3

2. Matthew 8:5-13

3. Matthew 8:23-27

4. Matthew 9:1-8

5. Matthew 12:11-13

6. Matthew 14:15-20

7. Mark 5:1-13

8. Mark 12:41-44

9. Luke 18:15-17

10. John 8:3-11

11. Think of a few circumstances in your life where God has spoken to you about His character and His ways. Remember, we always interpret circumstances through the

filter of God's Word and never interpret God's Word through the filter of our circumstances.

Chapter 5—God Speaks Through People

God's Messenger Boys

Let's look at a few examples of people God spoke to in the Old Testament.

1. God spoke to Moses.

   a. What precipitated God speaking to Moses? (Exodus 2:23-25)

   b. What did God say? (Exodus 3:1-10)

   c. What did Moses do next? (Exodus 4:18,29-31)

   d. What was the outcome of Moses' obedience? (Exodus 12:31)

   e. What might have been the outcome had Moses not listened to God's voice and obeyed?

2. God spoke to Joshua.

   a. What precipitated God speaking to Joshua? (Joshua 5:13)

   b. What did God say? (Joshua 6:1-5)

   c. What did Joshua do next? (Joshua 6:6-21)

   d. What was the outcome of Joshua's obedience? (Joshua 6:27)

   e. What might have been the outcome had Joshua not listened to God's voice and obeyed?

3. God spoke to Esther

   a. What precipitated God speaking to Esther? (Esther 3:8-11; 4:1-3)

   b. What did Mordecai urge Esther to do regarding the situation? (4:8)

c. Was she willing to follow his instructions? Explain. (4:9-11)

d. What was Mordecai's response to Esther's refusal? (4:12-14)

e. When Esther finally agreed to go before the king, what did she ask Mordecai to do? (4:15-16)

f. We do not know what God said to Esther during her time of prayer and fasting, but we know the actions she took at the end of those three days. Read the rest of the book of Esther and note the outcome of her obedience to God's voice. Especially look at 5:1-8; 7:1-6; 8:1-6; and 8:15.

g. What might have been the outcome had Esther not listened to God's voice and obeyed?

4. To sum up what you've learned about those who listen to God's voice, what was the ultimate outcome each time? Learning from Scripture, what can you expect when you listen and obey God's voice?

5. While God speaks through other people, we must always compare what others say to God's Word. What are some of the warnings that Peter gives us in this regard? (1 Peter 2:1-3,10-22)

Chapter 6—God Speaks Through Creation

A Picture Paints a Thousand Words

1. Read Romans 1:18-20. What does this tell you about how God speaks through creation?

2. How does God use the following creatures to teach us?

a. Proverbs 6:6

b. Proverbs 30:24-31

c. Isaiah 53:6

d. John 1:32-34

e. John 10:14

3. Now let's look at a situation with a bit of humor! Balaam and his talking mule. Read Numbers 22 and answer the following.

a. What was Balak's situation?

b. What did he want Balaam to do? (22:5-6)

c. What did God say to Balaam? (22:12-20)

d. Describe Balaam's encounter with the talking mule.

e. Do you find it interesting that Balaam didn't think it odd that his mule was talking?

f. What amazed Balaam more, the talking donkey or the angel?

g. What does Peter say about why God sent a talking donkey to stop the wayward prophet? (2 Peter 2:1-16)

Chapter 7—The World's Voice

As the World Turns

1. Read 1 Peter 1:13-16. How does Peter tell us to combat the desires of the world and the flesh? What is his charge to us?

2. What does Peter call our life before we come to Christ? (1 Peter 1:18)

3. What does King Solomon write about the life that we have when we seek God's wisdom? (Proverbs 8:33-35)

4. What does John tell us about what our attitude should be toward the world? (1 John 2:15)

5. The world's wisdom will come and go. Trends will change from season to season. Governments will legislate morality and change what is "acceptable" from year to year. But what does Peter tell us about the Word of God? (1 Peter 1:23) How does this relate to some of the Supreme Court or other legal decisions that have been made in our country over the past several decades?

6. Read 1 Peter 2:11. What does Peter call Christians in this verse? Have you ever felt like an alien because of how your beliefs conflict the world's beliefs around you? Explain.

7. What does Peter tell us others may think of us when we don't participate in the acceptable practices of the society? (1 Peter 4:4)

8. Sometimes our beliefs will be so opposed to the world's that we may find a bit of anger stirring in our souls. However, what does Peter tell us about how we are to approach those in the world with varying opinions? (1 Peter 1:15-16)

9. What warning does Paul give us about the wisdom of the world? (1 Corinthians 3:18-23).

10. Read Jesus' prayer for you and note everything He prayed in regard to you and the world. (John 17:6-25)

Chapter 8—Our Own Voice

It's All About Me

Let's compare two men in the Old Testament. One listened to his own voice, which said, "I can't do this," and the other listened to the echo of Jehovah, which said, "God can." As you reflect on each story, ponder which man you most resemble today and which man you long to resemble from this day forward.

1. Read Exodus 3:1-22.

   a. Describe Israel's dilemma in your own words.

   b. What was God's solution?

   c. What was Moses' reply to God's call on his life? (3:11; 3:13)

   d. Read Exodus 4:1-14 and note Moses' continued response to God. (4:1; 4:10; 4:13). Why was he afraid?

   e. How did God feel about Moses' lack of faith? (4:14)

   f. What was God's response to each of Moses' complaints?

2. Now let's look at David. Read 1 Samuel 17:1-58.

   a. Describe Israel's dilemma in your own words.

   b. Describe Goliath's physical appearance and demeanor.

   c. Who was David and what was his approximate age?

   d. What did David think about Goliath? (17:26)

   e. What was David's plan? Why was he not afraid? (17:32-37)

   f. How did Saul question David's confidence in God?

   g. What was Goliath's estimation of David? (17:41-44)

   h. Did David choose to listen to God's still, small voice or the voice of discouragement from Saul, his brothers, and Goliath?

3. The flesh says fear...God says faith. The flesh says, "I can't do it." God says, "I will do it for you." How do you see these two principles at work in the stories of Moses and David?

4. Notice which way Goliath fell (1 Samuel 17:49). If someone is hit in the forehead, which way would they normally fall? Any thoughts?

Chapter 9—The Deceiver's Voice

A Defeated Foe

While Satan is busy trying to mislead us, tempt us, and cause us to stumble, God gives us the assurance that we have the Holy Spirit in us to overcome anything the deceiver brings our way. Read the following verses and note what you learn about the victory that is ours.

1. John 16:11

2. Galatians 2:20

3. Colossians 2:15

4. Hebrews 2:14-15

5. 1 John 4:4

6. God has given us a battle plan for defeating the enemy. Read Ephesians 6:10-18.

   a. List the pieces of the armor of God and describe each one. You may want to draw a picture and label each piece. Notice what each piece covers. Also notice which pieces are for offensive and defensive use.

   b. The word "stand" is used several times in this passage. What imagery does that put in your mind?

   c. What do you learn from this passage about the importance of prayer in defeating the enemy?

Chapter 10—Low Dips of Emotion

Elijah Hits Rock Bottom

Read 1 Kings 18 and answer the following questions.

1. What did Elijah tell Ahab to do in verse 19?

2. What was his question to the people in verse 21?

3. Describe the scene in verses 22-29.

4. Describe the scene in verses 30-35.

5. How confident was Elijah that he had heard from God?

6. What happened after Elijah prayed? (verse 38)

Before we move to the next passage, summarize what you've learned about Elijah's courage, confidence in God, capacity to hear God's voice, and physical stamina.

In chapter 19, Elijah takes a sudden turn for the worse. Read 1 Kings 19 and answer the following questions.

7. What made the courageous Elijah shudder with fear?

8. What sign of depression or discouragement do you see in Elijah?

9. What question did God ask Elijah? (verses 9,13)

10. Do you think God told Elijah to run and hide from Jezebel? Why do you think he ran?

11. What did Elijah do after he heard God's voice in the gentle whisper?

12. Do you see a correlation between Elijah's sudden lack of faith and the timing of God appointing a new prophet?

13. Why is it important to learn from the examples of men and women in the Bible? (James 5:17)

Elijah was a man who heard God's voice, but then one woman's threats caused him to sink into a depression and give up. Have you ever had a time in your life when you allowed negative comments from someone to impair your faith? If so, explain.

The next time you run in fear, or hide because of doubts, remember God's words to Elijah: "What are you doing here?"

Chapter 11—Tall Walls of Sin

Roadblocks and Detours

One of the great stories of the Bible is Moses and his journey to the Promised Land. Along the way, the people of Israel floundered between listening to God and not listening to God. Also, their sin caused God to have times of silence. Let's look at a couple of those times.

1. Read Numbers chapter 12 and answer the following questions.

   a. Who was Miriam and what was her primary "job" in leading the people out of Egypt and to the Promised Land? (Exodus 15:20-21)

   b. What did she do to cause God to become angry? (Numbers 12:1)

   c. What was God's response to her jealousy and gossip? (Numbers 12:2-12)

   d. How long did Miriam have leprosy? (12:15)

   e. What did the people of Israel have to do during that time? Did they continue their journey or stop and wait?

   f. Have you ever experienced a time when you felt that God responded to your sin as He did in verse 9?

   g. Have you ever experienced a time when other people's progress was impeded by your sin?

2. In the Old Testament, the Holy of Holies was a place in the tabernacle where only the High Priest could go. A curtain separated man from the presence of God. Before the high priest presented himself, he had to go through extensive cleansing rituals. Even then, he tied a rope around his ankle that was held by someone on the outside to pull him out in case he died in God's presence.

a. What happened to that dividing curtain when Jesus died on the cross? (Mark 15:38)

b. What was the direction of the tear?

c. Who do you think tore the curtain?

d. Because of Jesus' sacrifice for our sin, how are we to approach God? (Ephesians 3:12; Hebrews 10:19-22)

e. What is the promise of Hebrews 10:32-39?

Chapter 12—Spiritual Depletion

The Not so Young and Restless

Sometimes God causes us to have a restless spirit when He's trying to get our attention. This was the case with several men and women in the Bible. Let's take a look at a few examples.

1. Look at Esther 6.

a. What prompted the king to ask for the book of records of the chronicles?

b. What did the king discover?

c. How did this restlessness save Mordecai's life?

2. Samuel was one of the mightiest prophets in the Old Testament. It is no wonder one of his first assignments was to learn how to hear God's voice. Read 1 Samuel 3:4-10 and describe what happened. What were the words Samuel finally spoke to God in verse 10?

3. Read Genesis 32:22-28. Did Jacob have a good night's sleep on this occasion? What happened to him?

4. Why did Pilate's wife warn him not to condemn Jesus? (Matthew 27:19)

5. Can you think of a time when you were restless and later discovered that God was trying to get your attention? Explain.

6. God may cause restlessness in our spirits when He's trying to get our attention. He also gives us peace when we listen to His voice. Read the following verses and record what you learn about the peace we can experience when we become women who listen to God.

   a. John 14:27

   b. Philippians 4:7

   c. Colossians 3:15

Chapter 13—Retracted Antennas

The Choice Is Ours

1. Read Isaiah 50:2 and Jeremiah 6:17. What was God's complaint in both of these references?

2. What did God say about the Israelites? (Jeremiah 7:21-28; 13:10)

3. From the following verses, what are the results of not listening to God?

   a. Deuteronomy 1:43-45

   b. 2 Chronicles 24:19-20

   c. Nehemiah 9:29-30

   d. Jeremiah 25:7

   e. Jeremiah 26:4-6

4. Do you think a person can worship the Lord and still not listen to His voice? What did the writer of 2 Kings 17:34-40 say about the people of Israel?

5. What was Jesus' warning and promise to those who listen? (Luke 8:18)

6. Jesus was a man who always had His spiritual antenna raised. Sometimes it is easy to forget that while Jesus was fully God, He was also fully man. He experienced hunger, thirst, longing, hurt, disappointment, elation, sadness, temptation, pain, anger, and fatigue. And on any given day, in order to know what He was to do and say, He had to be a man who listened to God.

   Read the following verses and note what Jesus said about the words He spoke.
   a. John 7:16-17
   b. John 8:25,28
   c. John 14:10
   d. John 15:15
   e. John 17:8

7. Read the following verses and note what Jesus said about His actions.
   a. John 5:19
   b. John 5:30
   c. John 6:38
   d. John 14:31

8. Read John 6:16-17. Where do you think Jesus was? What do you think He was doing?

9. Read Mark 1:35-38. Where was Jesus? What was He doing? Explain His confident response to the disciples' request.

10. Why did Jesus go through Samaria? (John 4:4) What do you think it means "had to go"?

11. How do you think spending time alone with God each day would affect your ability to hear His voice?

12. Can you think of a period of time in your life when you were most tuned in to God's voice? (That may be now.) If so, do you see any correlation between your spiritual acuity and time spent alone with Him?

Chapter 14—Unbelief

Believe It or Not

We should never fall into the false belief that if we believe something hard enough, God will do what we want Him to do. Faith is important, and without it we cannot please God (Hebrews 11:6), but faith in God is not to be confused with an ability to control God.

1. Read Daniel 3:8-30 and answer the following questions.

   a. What did Shadrach, Meshach, and Abednego refuse to do?

   b. What was their punishment?

   c. What was their reply to the king? (verses 16-18)

   d. Were they certain that God would save them from the fire?

   e. What was the king's response to this miracle? (verses 28-29)

   f. By the way, how many men did the king see in the furnace? (verse 25) Who do you think was in the fire with the three young men?

2. Now let's look at two more men who believed God. Read Numbers 13:1-33.

   a. What were the two opposing reports?

   b. Whom did the Israelites believe? (14:1-4)

   c. Joshua and Caleb believed God and entered the Promised Land many years later, but what happened to the entire generation that did not believe God? (14:23)

   d. One of the women to enter the Promised Land was not an Israelite. What was her profession?

   e. What did she believe about God? (Joshua 2:9)

   f. What was the result of Rahab's belief in God? (Joshua 6:22)

Chapter 15—Preparing to Listen to God

Speak, Lord, I'm Listening

1. Read Luke 18:11-14.

   a. What was the first man's problem?

   b. How was the second man different?

   c. What did Jesus say about the two men, and how does that relate to us?

2. How does James tell us to receive the Word of God? (James 1:21) What does that mean to you?

3. Compare the attitude of Simon the Pharisee with the woman caught in adultery. Who received God's blessing and heard His voice? (Luke 7:36-50)

Today we're going to do something a bit different. We're going to have an exercise in meditating on God's Word in order to move it from our heads to our hearts. Turn to the familiar passage known as The Lord's Prayer (Matthew 6:9-15). We're going to read this passage one word or phrase at a time and humbly pray that God will speak to us through His Word.

> *Lord, as we come to You now, I pray that You will open the eyes of our hearts to see Your words with fresh eyes. Illumine our minds to understand the rich truths in this passage as You opened the minds of Your disciples after Jesus' resurrection. In Jesus' name, amen.*

1. Read the first line of the Lord's prayer. Now go back and meditate on the word "our." What does that encompass? Who is "our"? Ask God to give you special insight and note what He says to you.

   Our

2. Move to the word "Father." What does that mean to you? What does it mean to be invited to address God as your Father? What does a perfect "father" look like? Meditate on the word "father" and ask God to give you special insight and note what He says to you.

   Father

Now follow the same pattern throughout the passage. Stop to meditate and pray over each word of each phrase. Ask God to speak to your heart and give you insight into the passage. He may lead you to other verses. Note what you "hear."

   in heaven

   hallowed (holy)

   be your name

   Your kingdom

   come

   Your will

   be done

on earth

as it is in heaven

Give us

this day

our daily

bread

Forgive us

our debts

as we forgive our debtors

And lead us not

into temptation

but deliver us

from the evil one

I hope this has been a beneficial exercise for you. What is a reward of meditating on God's Word? (Joshua 1:8)

Chapter 16—Blessings of Listening to God

Friend to Friend

Let's end our journey by looking at a few men and women in the New Testament who had the privilege of being spoken to by God.

1. Read Matthew 1:18-25.

   a. How did God speak to Joseph?

   b. What did God say?

   c. What was Joseph's response?

   d. What would have been the probable result had Joseph not listened to God?

2. Read Acts 8:26-40.

   a. What did God instruct Philip to do?

b. What was his response?

c. What was the outcome of Philip listening to God?

3. Read Acts 9:1-19.

    a. How did God speak to Saul?

    b. What did God say?

    c. What was Saul's response?

    d. How have we benefited because Saul listened to God?

4. One of the greatest blessings of knowing Jesus Christ as Savior is that He calls us friends.

    a. Read and record John 15:15.

    b. Compare your conversations with a stranger or acquaintance in the grocery store with your conversations with a close friend. How do they differ?

    c. Thinking of that continuum, where does your relationship with God fall?

•_____•

cordial   intimate

    d. Where do you want it to be?

    e. What are you willing to do to develop intimacy with God?

On page 244, write a prayer of commitment to God expressing your desire to become a woman who listens to Him.

NOTES

God Still Speaks Today

1. Henry T. Blackaby and Claude V. King, *Experiencing God* (Nashville, TN: The Sunday School Board of the Southern Baptist Convention, 1990), p. 15.

2. Ken Gire, *The Reflective Life* (Colorado Springs: Chariot Victor Publishing, 1998), p. 23.

Chapter 1—God Speaks Through His Word

1. W.E. Vine, Merrill F. Unger, and William White Jr., *Vine's Complete Expository Dictionary of Old and New Testament Words* (Nashville, TN: Thomas Nelson, 1985), p. 683.

2. John Newton, *John Newton: Letters of a Slave Trader* (Chicago: Moody Bible Institute, 1983), pp. 69-70.

3. Geoffrey C. Ward with Ric Burns and Ken Burns, *The Civil War* (New York: Alfred A. Knopf, Inc., 1998), pp. 82-83. Punctuation in Sullivan Ballou's letter was amended slightly for clarity.

4. Gire, *The Reflective Life,* p. 69.

Chapter 2—God Speaks Through the Holy Spirit

1. Vine, et al., *Vine's Complete Expository Dictionary of Old and New Testament Words*, p. 111.

2. Ibid., p. 111.

3. Gire, *The Reflective Life,* p. 71.

Chapter 3—God Speaks Through Prayer

1. David McCasland, *Oswald Chambers: Abandoned to God* (Grand Rapids, MI: Discovery House Publishers, 1993), p. 110.

Chapter 4—God Speaks Through Circumstances

1. Henry and Richard Blackaby, *Hearing God's Voice* (Nashville, TN: Broadman and Holman Publishers, 2002), p. 140.
2. Frederick Buechner, *A Room Called Remember* (San Francisco: Harper and Row Publishers, 1984), p. 13.
3. Frederick Buechner, *The Magnificent Defeat* (San Francisco: Harper and Row Publishers, 1966), pp. 48-49.
4. Gire, *The Reflective Life*, p. 125.
5. Blackaby and King, *Experiencing God*, p. 15.
6. Charles Stanley, *How to Listen to God* (Nashville, TN: Thomas Nelson, 1985), p. 40.

Chapter 5—God Speaks Through People

1. Blackaby and King, *Experiencing God,* p. 25.
2. Henry and Richard Blackaby, *Hearing God's Voice,* p. 199.

Chapter 6—God Speaks Through Creation

1. Beth Moore, *Jesus, the One and Only* (Nashville, TN: Lifeway Press, 2000), pp. 41-42.
2. W.Y. Fullerton, *Charles Haddon Spurgeon: London's Most Popular Preacher* (Chicago: Moody Bible Institute, 1966), p. 197.
3. A.W. Tozer, *The Pursuit of God* (Camp Hill, PA: Christina Publications, Inc., 1982), pp. 80-81.
4. Carole Mayhall, "Listening to God," in Judith Couchman, ed., *One Holy Passion* (Colorado Springs, CO: WaterBrook, 1998), p. 210.
5. Robert J. Morgan, *Nelson's Complete Book of Stories, Illustrations, and Quotes* (Nashville, TN: Thomas Nelson, Inc., 2000), p. 369.

Chapter 7—The World's Voice

1. Kenneth Boa, *Conformed to His Image* (Grand Rapids, MI: Zondervan, 2001), p. 336.

Chapter 8—Our Own Voice

1. Sharon Jaynes and Lysa TerKeurst, *A Woman's Secret to a Balanced Life* (Eugene, OR: Harvest House, 2004).

Chapter 9—The Deceiver's Voice

1. Sharon Jaynes, *Ultimate Makeover: Becoming Spiritually Beautiful in Christ* (Chicago: Moody Publishing, 2003), p. 120.
2. Neil Anderson, *The Bondage Breaker* (Eugene, OR: Harvest House, 1990), p. 23.

Chapter 12—Spiritual Depletion

1. *NIV Study Bible* (Grand Rapids, MI: Zondervan Publishing House, 1995), p. 1800.

Chapter 14—Unbelief

1. Pamela J. Johnson, "Kentucky Truck Driver Answers Prayers of Nation," *Orlando Sentinel* (October 25, 2002), p. A14.

2. Kenneth L. Barker and John R. Kohlenberger III, *Zondervan NIV Commentary: Volume 2* (Grand Rapids, MI: Zondervan Publishing Corporation, 1994), p. 96.

Chapter 15—Preparing to Listen to God

1. Anne Morrow Lindbergh, *Gift from the Sea* (New York: Pantheon Books, 1955), pp. 29-30.

2. Fullerton, *Charles Haddon Spurgeon: London's Most Popular Preacher,* p. 99.

3. Adapted from Stephen R. Covey, *First Things First* (New York: Simon & Schuster, 1994), pp. 88-89.

4. J.I. Packer, as quoted by Charles Stanley, *How to Listen to God* (Nashville, TN: Thomas Nelson, Inc., 1985), p. 94.

5. Vine, et al., *Vine's Complete Expository Dictionary of Old and New Testament Words*, p. 150.

6. Gire, *The Reflective Life,* p. 90.

7. Excerpted in *The Growing Disciple*, The 2:7 Series, Course 1 (Colorado Springs, CO: NavPress, 1987), pp. 69-73.

8. Thomas Merton, *Seeds of Contemplation* (New York: New Directions Publishers, 1949), p. 17.

9. Gire, *The Reflective Life*, p. 120.

Chapter 16—Blessings of Listening to God

1. Taken from *Have You Heard of the Four Spiritual Laws?* by Bill Bright. Copyright 1965, 1994, New Life Publications, Campus Crusade for Christ. All rights reserved. Used by permission.

2. Oswald Chambers, *My Utmost for His Highest: Updated Edition* (Grand Rapids, MI: Discovery House Publishers), June 8.

3. Ibid., October 10.

4. Ibid., June 15.

5. Ibid., November 2.

Standing at the Crossroads

1. Chambers, *My Utmost for His Highest,* January 1.

About the Author

Sharon Jaynes is an international inspirational speaker and Bible teacher for women's conferences and events. She is the author of several books, including *Becoming the Woman of His Dreams, Your Scars Are Beautiful to God, Becoming Spiritually Beautiful, "I'm Not Good Enough"...and Other Lies Women Tell Themselves,* and *Listening to God Day by Day.* Her books have been translated into several foreign languages and impact women around the globe. Her passion is to encourage, equip, and empower women to walk in courage and confidence as they grasp their true identity as a child of God and a co-heir with Christ.

Sharon is a cofounder of Girlfriends in God, a conference and online ministry that crosses denominational, racial, and generational boundaries to unify the body of Christ. To learn more visit www.girlfriendsinGod.com.

Sharon and her husband, Steve, have one grown son, Steven. They call North Carolina home.

Sharon is always honored to hear from her readers. You can contact her directly at Sharon@sharonjaynes.com or at her mailing address:

Sharon Jaynes
PO Box 725
Matthews, NC 28106

To learn more about Sharon's books and speaking ministry or to inquire about having her speak at your next event, visit www.sharonjaynes.com.

Other Books by Sharon Jaynes

LISTENING TO GOD DAY BY DAY

How do ordinary days become filled with extraordinary moments? When people listen to God's still, small voice and see His fingerprints on the pages of their lives. These stories will enable you to see how God is moving in the lives of fellow travelers and to recognize God's presence in your own life.

THE POWER OF A WOMAN'S WORDS

The Power of a Woman's Words is for every woman who desires to use her words to build up rather than tear down, to encourage rather than discourage, to cheer rather than jeer. It is for all who desire to have more control over that mighty force called the tongue.

WHAT GOD REALLY THINKS ABOUT WOMEN

With her trademark biblical perspective, Sharon Jaynes explores how God interacted with and cared for women of the Bible and uncovers surprising insights she is excited to share with you today—God has great dreams for women and continues to transform them, heart by heart, in deeply personal ways.

THE 5 DREAMS OF EVERY WOMAN...
AND HOW GOD WANTS TO FULFILL THEM

Sharon shares powerful stories alongside biblical, compassionate guidance to help restore women's hope in love, marriage, motherhood, purpose, and more. You will learn to give your longings and brokenness to God and delight in His renewal and remarkable dreams for you. Study questions included.

BECOMING SPIRITUALLY BEAUTIFUL

In *Becoming Spiritually Beautiful,* Sharon gently shares how becoming spiritually beautiful is something full of promise and possibilities. Spiritual beauty brings new beginnings, fresh faith, and the hope of a beauty unique in the universe.

Other Good
Harvest House Reading

THE POWER OF A PRAYING® WOMAN
by *Stormie Omartian*

Stormie's deep knowledge of Scripture and candid examples from her own prayer life provide guidance for women who seek to trust God with deep longings and cover every area of life with prayer.

SMALL CHANGES FOR A BETTER LIFE
by *Elizabeth George*

What is God's best for a woman's life, and how can she live it out? These questions are answered in this uplifting book by bestselling author Elizabeth George. Women will find dozens of highly practical tips for every area of daily life—in their marriages, families, homes, and places of work and in their friendships, health, finances, and personal growth.

BECOMING A WOMAN OF EXTRAORDINARY FAITH
by *Julie Clinton*

Julie Clinton, author, speaker, and president of Extraordinary Women, offers an engaging 10-week journey to embrace biblical principles, inspired priorities, and refueled purpose as you gather the riches of the extraordinary life including healing, grace, strengthened relationships, and a clear understanding of God's Word and hope for your path.

A WOMAN'S SECRET FOR CONFIDENT LIVING
by *Karol Ladd*

Bestselling author Karol Ladd shares powerful truths from Colossians and reveals an exciting path to confident living through God's grace. With an inspiring belief in God's purpose for each woman and insightful study questions, Karol helps individuals and groups experience their God-confidence through transformed perspectives, relationships, thoughts, and dreams.

HARVEST HOUSE PUBLISHERS